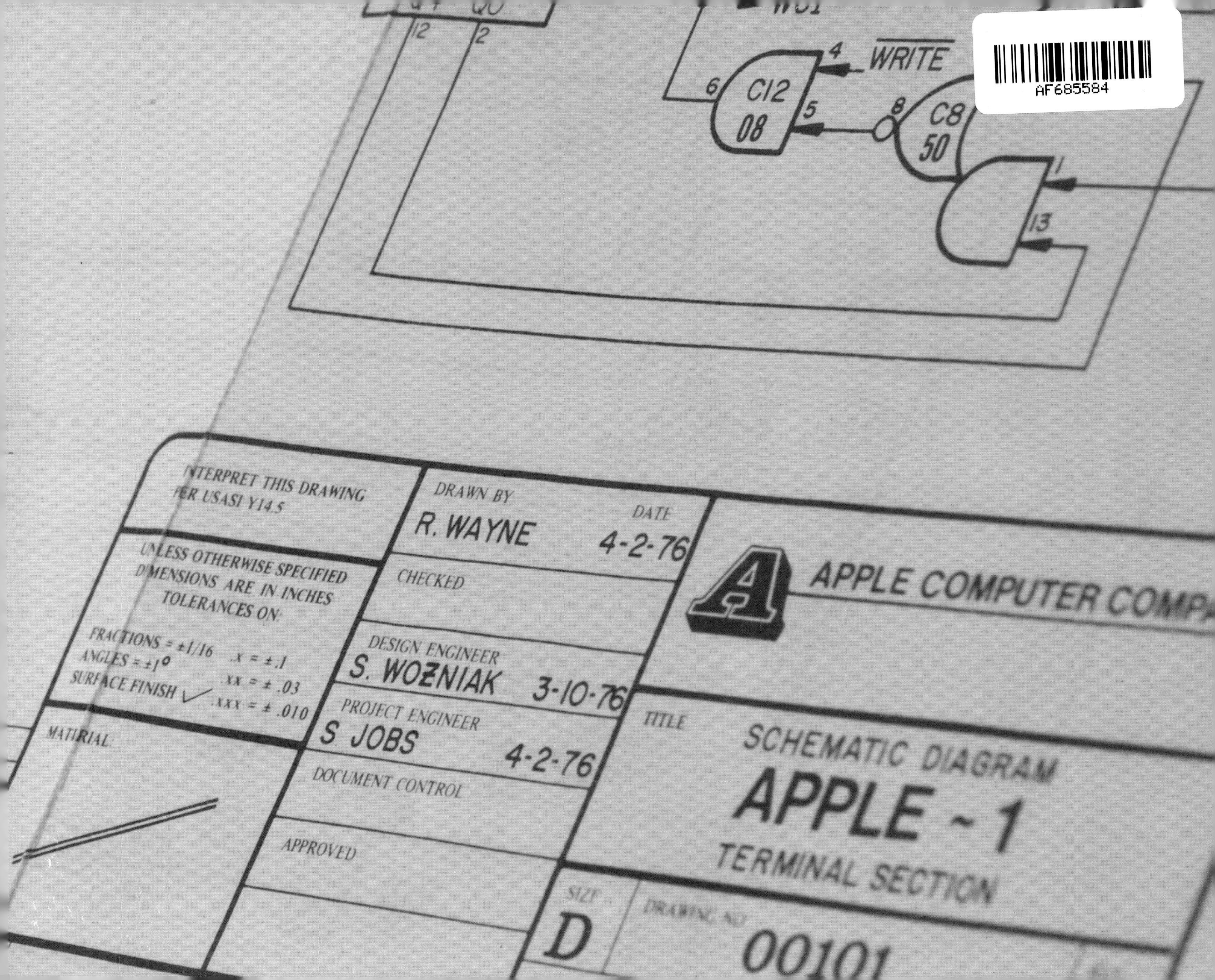

12
2
WRITE
4
6
C12
08
5
8
C8
50
1
13
INTERPRET THIS DRAWING
PER USASI Y14.5
UNLESS OTHERWISE SPECIFIED
DIMENSIONS ARE IN INCHES
TOLERANCES ON:
FRACTIONS = ±1/16 .x = ±.1
ANGLES = ±1°
.xx = ± .03
SURFACE FINISH
.xxx = ± .010
MATERIAL:
DRAWN BY
R. WAYNE
DATE
4-2-76
CHECKED
DESIGN ENGINEER
S. WOZNIAK
3-10-76
PROJECT ENGINEER
S. JOBS
4-2-76
DOCUMENT CONTROL
APPROVED
APPLE COMPUTER COMPA
TITLE
SCHEMATIC DIAGRAM
APPLE ~ 1
TERMINAL SECTION
SIZE
D
DRAWING NO
00101

ICONIC

SPRAGUE

ICONIC

A Photographic Tribute to Apple Innovation

JONATHAN ZUFI

LIBRARY OF CONGRESS PCN 2013905520

ISBN-0-9885817-0-8

Printed in China

Principle photography by Jonathan Zufi
Photo editing and additional photography by Forest McMullin
Design by Lisa Clark
Editing by Shelley Holloway of Holloway House

Photo: Apple Headquarters (right) Herb Lingl, Aerial Archives (aerialarchives.com)
Photo: iPod (pages188/189) Kyle Burdg
Photo: Macintosh Prototype (pages 242/243) Mark Richards
with permission from the Computer History Museum (http://www.computerhistory.org)

6 5 4 3 2 1

RIDGEWOOD PUBLISHING
Atlanta, Georgia
www.ridgewoodpublishing.com

This book is dedicated to all Apple employees—past, present, and future, on behalf of the millions of loyal fans around the world.

Apple's corporate offices in Cupertino, California ▸

Contents

Foreword by Jim Dalrymple

There is something very special about Steve Jobs and the people he brought together. It was the perfect combination of a man who could seemingly predict what people wanted before they knew it and a group of people that shared a passion for designing the best products in the world.

The result is, of course, Apple. The impact of the designs and products that these people envisioned has changed entire industries. They changed the way the world thinks products should work and how we interact with them.

It's an incredible feat to design and manufacture a product that revolutionizes an industry. In fact, it's rare that a company can claim to have transformed even one industry in its entire history. Those are special companies. They become household names. And, in certain exceptional cases, etching the essence of their brand into the foundation of society, they become . . . iconic.

Apple has done this no less than six times, perhaps more if you look at its software innovations. The Macintosh, iPod, iPhone, iPad, digital music distribution, digital video distribution with movies and TV programming—Apple has changed them all. The products that Apple released in these markets weren't just deemed popular by consumers, they became the standard by which all other products were judged.

Though Apple has made billions of dollars, that wasn't its first priority. It was excellence in design and having that design help consumers solve problems. That's one of the secrets to the company's continued success.

Apple identifies a need and solves a problem. By ensuring that the driving factor in making a product is the quality of the hardware and software design, Apple has continually led the industries it enters.

Apple has proven over the years that it is not afraid to step outside the current design philosophies to make something better, something that helps us enjoy technology, or be more productive, all without adding complexity—more often reducing it.

That may sound easy, but it's really not. It takes the foresight of a visionary like Steve Jobs, the innate brilliance of an engineering savant like Steve Wozniak, and a host of like-minded engineers and designers to make it happen. A team with tireless initiative willing to dedicate themselves to their mutual goals.

There are many companies that design powerful products that help us in our day-to-day lives. Whether it's for work or pleasure, there are applications and hardware devices that make every task in our day a little bit easier. That's why we love technology so much.

Unfortunately, many of the new technology products are very difficult to use—in many cases, needlessly so. That is why we also tend to hate technology. This is why I believe Apple has been so successful. When the design of your product is so simple that it appeals to everyone from children to seniors and is powerful enough to help run governments and aid in scientific research, you know you've done something right.

Steve Jobs pushed his employees to be the absolute best they could be. He accepted nothing less from himself or the people around him. He applauded and scolded the people that he worked with, but there is nobody else that could inspire so many people with the desire to change so many industries.

The decisions to make and release a product at Apple are different from those at many other companies. Instead of asking how much money they can make by releasing a product, Apple asks how they can solve a problem. The starting point for Apple is completely different from any other company's, so it's only natural that it ends up in a different place too. In my opinion, a much better place.

The ability to hide the complexity of a product's capabilities behind a simple design is not something that every company can do. That is something special. It takes special people, dedicated to making the best products, using the best materials, and doing it to solve a problem or fulfill a need shared by many. And in making it simple, Apple is able to bring beauty to its products, both inside and out.

—J. D.

Foreword by Steve Wozniak

My history with Apple has been almost life-long, preceded by what I thought would be a life-long position at Hewlett-Packard—a company that lived by the philosophy of community, treating its employees with respect. Everything was open to thought, discussion, and innovation. The environment allowed me to be me, doing what I loved . . . for the fun of it.

When I left HP for Apple, I had visions of being part of that same type of community, joining a creative, driven team of engineers and designers whose passion for building was equal to mine, where we would be able to spend every day thinking about the product, not the business. My life was engineering, and I wanted everyone we hired to have that same drive and experience the same exhilaration I felt when I created the Apple II. To this day, I am so proud of the fact that not one bug was ever found in the hardware or software of that computer. Not one. That's because I lived it. It was in my head. It was a part of me.

Apple has grown a bit since those early days, and has had many successes and a few missteps along the way. But no one at the company really viewed any of the less successful products as failures. Every product built has been integral to the journey. Apple has learned from each of them and is now better for it. The Apple products themselves are what have attracted the many loyal users and fans, but the lion's share of Apple's success can be attributed to its secret formula: attracting dedicated, creative people driven by the desire to create innovative, forward-thinking products for today's technology-driven consumers.

From the hardware that lies beneath the sleek designs, to the equally innovative packaging, Apple teams look beyond today, and even tomorrow. Their talent is anticipating not only what will best serve customers' needs, but what will prove to be irresistible—ultimately inspiring loyalty to all things Apple.

When Jonathan showed me an early draft of *Iconic*, memories of the many amazing products that have come out of Apple, as well as some of the incredible engineers and designers I worked with over the years, came flooding back.

The beauty of design that Apple is known for deserves beautiful photography, and that is what Jonathan has given us. Within these pages, Jonathan presents a thoughtful and artistic gift to Apple fans and employees alike: photographs of Apple products—from hardware to packaging—the likes of which I've never seen compiled before. Jonathan's passion for this project is reflected on every page, and each honors the hard work of every employee and collaborator that has passed through Apple's doors.

—Steve Wozniak
Co-founder, Apple Inc.

ICONIC

Introduction by Jonathan Zufi

Do you remember your first Apple product? I'm sure it wasn't your last. Which is your favorite? What generation is it? Did you know Apple made printers? Scanners? Cameras? The breadth of products Apple has offered over the years may surprise you.

My first exposure to Apple was in my high school science class in Melbourne, Australia in 1982. Apple Logo and pure 6802 assembly were my first endeavors into software development, and my first game on the Apple II was RobotWars. Years later, feeling a bit nostalgic, I decided to search for a copy of the game and an old Apple II on which to play it. As I browsed through the countless specimens of vintage Apple gear on eBay, it became apparent that there was no truly extensive, high-definition photographic repository of Apple products . . . anywhere.

What was I to do? Though photographically challenged and a family man with a full-time day job, I built *Shrine of Apple* (shrineofapple.com) as my outlet for the world to see, appreciate, and enjoy the beauty and breadth of Apple.

Purchasing over 500 unique pieces of Apple hardware (many in their original packaging) was no simple task. Next was learning how to shoot professional images of these products, ultimately capturing over 150,000. But once I'd selected the best of them and created the website, I realized that having this beautiful photography trapped inside a digital display meant the viewer wasn't getting the full richness the photographs had to offer. So, the idea of *Iconic* was born. It isn't a reference book of every Apple product ever made. It is a tribute with thoughtfully selected images that I believe highlight what Apple truly is. Iconic.

During the four years I worked on this project, I met some amazing people, each integral to the story I was telling. One of those people was Bill Fernandez, Apple's first full-time employee. He told me about his team's motivation, what drove them. He said their goal was to make the Macintosh something their families and friends would love to have. As I interviewed others at Apple, it became apparent that this is at the core of all Apple does. They create and build things their families will love to hold, use, and enjoy. Having spoken to countless former Apple employees, another constant was the fond memories they have of their time at Apple. I hope what I have built does their memories—and their craft—justice.

When I began my project, the world was unaware of the true severity of Steve Job's illness. The impact of his absence—to our community and the world—has been great. I believe his passion, vision, and drive are reflected in this tribute, dedicated not only to the company he built, but to the people who are Apple. My project now complete, I wish he could have seen it.

At the end of each new product introduction, Steve would always thank the Apple employees for working so hard, and for so long, on the product he had just introduced to the world. I would like thank those very same people, without whom we wouldn't have the Apple we all know today, and I wouldn't have been inspired to create this book to share with everyone connected to Apple—customers, as well as employees, past and present.

Steve Jobs once said: "I want Apple's design not just to be the best in the computer industry, but to be the very best in the entire world." I believe that Apple has reached this goal, and will continue to hold that crown for many years to come.

—*J. Z.*

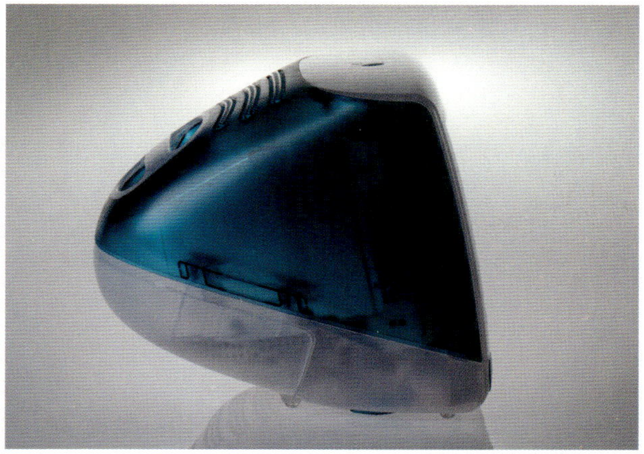

Daniel Kottke, *engineer, entrepreneur, former Apple Employee #12*

It is dizzying to think about the evolution of computer hardware that has taken place over the last four decades, and how much technology has progressed since those early days in 1976 when we were plugging ICs (integrated circuits) into the Apple I in the Jobs' garage. The Apple I now seems as primitive as the Model T.

Working on your computer's printed circuit board (PCB) thirty-seven years ago was easy—everything was socketed. That meant you could always fix a board, if you had the parts to swap against it. Those days are long gone. The current paradigm for Apple is to put all of the electronics into the flat-screen display. This revolution has resulted in the boon in availability and popularity of tablets, as well as sleek new notebook designs that also take advantage of today's cloud storage. Apple's innovative leadership in these areas is noteworthy, but, alas, what is to become of the venerable desktop computer that started us on this lovefest?

Professional programmers will always need a fully capable machine, but for most of us, the "computer" we've come to know is quickly being integrated into your big-screen TV, or held in your hand. Today, our world seems to be driven by mobile computing. The per-capita data foretells the possibility that the desktop's popularity has passed its prime. Every day, more and more people are moving away from the desktop in favor of a notebook. Popular opinion seems to be that, between a smartphone, a tablet, and the cloud, today's technology consumers no longer have need for a desktop machine, or even a notebook. I disagree.

As evidenced by Apple's latest iMac, the company is not giving up on it. In fact, Apple is making it all but irresistible. I remember the days of the Macintosh, and yes, we all loved it. It was a great piece of machinery, and I am proud of my contributions to that period in Apple's history. But, when you see the sleek beauty and the engineering genius that recently brought us the 2012 iMac with its ultra-thin display, it will be clear: the Apple desktop hasn't seen the end of its reign.

DESKTOPS

7.5K
7.5K
7404
(6800 ONLY)
2519
Apple Computer 1
Palo Alto, Ca. Copyright 1976
47

Apple I, 1976 ▼

7605
320 MP-12

"Without the Apple I, nothing would have followed.
There wouldn't have been an iPhone if there hadn't been an Apple I."

—Bill Fernandez, Apple's first full-time employee

Apple I, 1976

"I knew the Apple II was great when I bought it, but as I dug into the details, it just completely blew me away the creative artistic approach that the designers had taken."

—Andy Hertzfeld, member of the original Macintosh development team

Apple II J-Plus, 1978 ▸

Apple II, 1980 ▸

apple II
j-plus
RESET
REPT
RETURN
BELL

apple
IIc
ESC

"After being part of the Atari 800 Group, I finally broke down and bought an Apple IIe to analyze the competition. I found that I enjoyed the Apple and all the available software so much that I became an Apple enthusiast."

—**Nolan Bushnell, Founder of Atari**

◂ Apple IIe, 1983

▼ Bell & Howell Apple II, 1979 ▸

" 2
3
$ 4
% 5
& 6
' 7
(8
) 9
Q
W
E
R
T
Y
U
I
O
A
S
D
F
BELL G
H
J
K
Z
X
C
V
B
ESC
CTRL

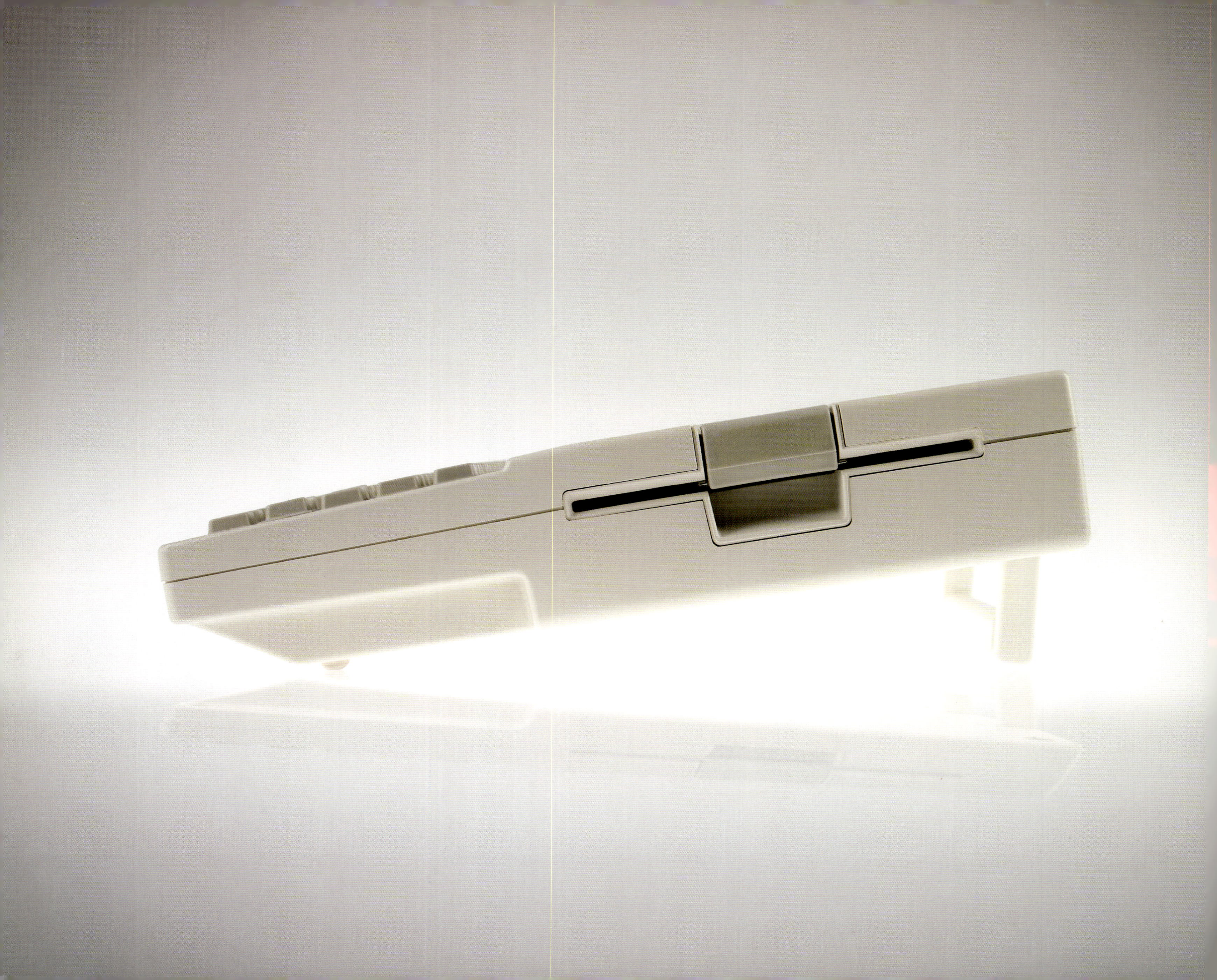

"Design is a funny word. Some people think design means how it looks . . . To design something really well, you have to get it. You have to really grok what it's all about. It takes a passionate commitment to really thoroughly understand something, chew it up, not just quickly swallow it."

—Steve Jobs, Co-founder, Apple Inc.

◂ Apple IIc, 1984; Apple IIc Plus, 1988 ▸

monitor ///
ON
apple ///

◂ Apple III, 1980

◂ Apple IIGS,1986

◂ Apple Lisa 2, 1984 ▸

Reset
Video Out
Parallel Device
Mouse
Serial Device A
Serial Device B
PARALLEL PORT
6522 KEYBOARD
BATTERY
MADE IN
© 1982

"This is Lisa. It's the only personal system of its kind ... Lisa follows the way you actually work in the office. It's not another personal computer. It's a personal office system. And it's nothing short of a revolution."

—Lisa marketing material, 1982

▾ Apple Lisa 2, 1984 ▸

Backspace
Clear
–
7
8
+
*
4
9
5
/
1
6
2
,
3
.
Enter

"When we were designing the Macintosh, we talked amongst ourselves about an ethos . . .

▲ left to right: Mac 128K, 1984; Mac 512Ke, 1986; Macintosh Plus, 1986; Macintosh SE, 1987

We were building the computer that we were not only willing but desirous of inflicting on our loved ones."

—Bill Fernandez

▲ left to right: Macintosh Classic II, 1991; Macintosh Performa 200, 1992; Macintosh Color Classic, 1993; Macintosh Color Classic II, 1993

Macintosh Plus, 1986 ▸

Backspace
Clear
7
8
9
Return

> "I remember when I turned on my first Mac. The intro video sequence came on with the fun music, and I instantly knew that I had invested in a company that cared very deeply about its customers." —**Alex Heath, writer**

◂ Macintosh Color Classic II, 1993; Macintosh SE, 1987 ▸

Macintosh SE

"The Apple I was the start, the Macintosh was the fruition of an amazing quest for excellence."

—Gabreal Franklin, Encore Systems, creator of MacWrite

◂ Macintosh Plus, 1986; Mac 128K, 1984 ▸

"...Apple's first brochure [said] 'Simplicity is the Ultimate Sophistication.' [We meant] when you first attack a problem it seems really simple because you don't understand it....When you start to really understand it, you come up with these very complicated solutions...Most people stop there. But a few people keep burning the midnight oil and finally understand the underlying principles of the problem and come up with an elegantly simple solution for it. But very few people go the distance to get there."

—Steve Jobs

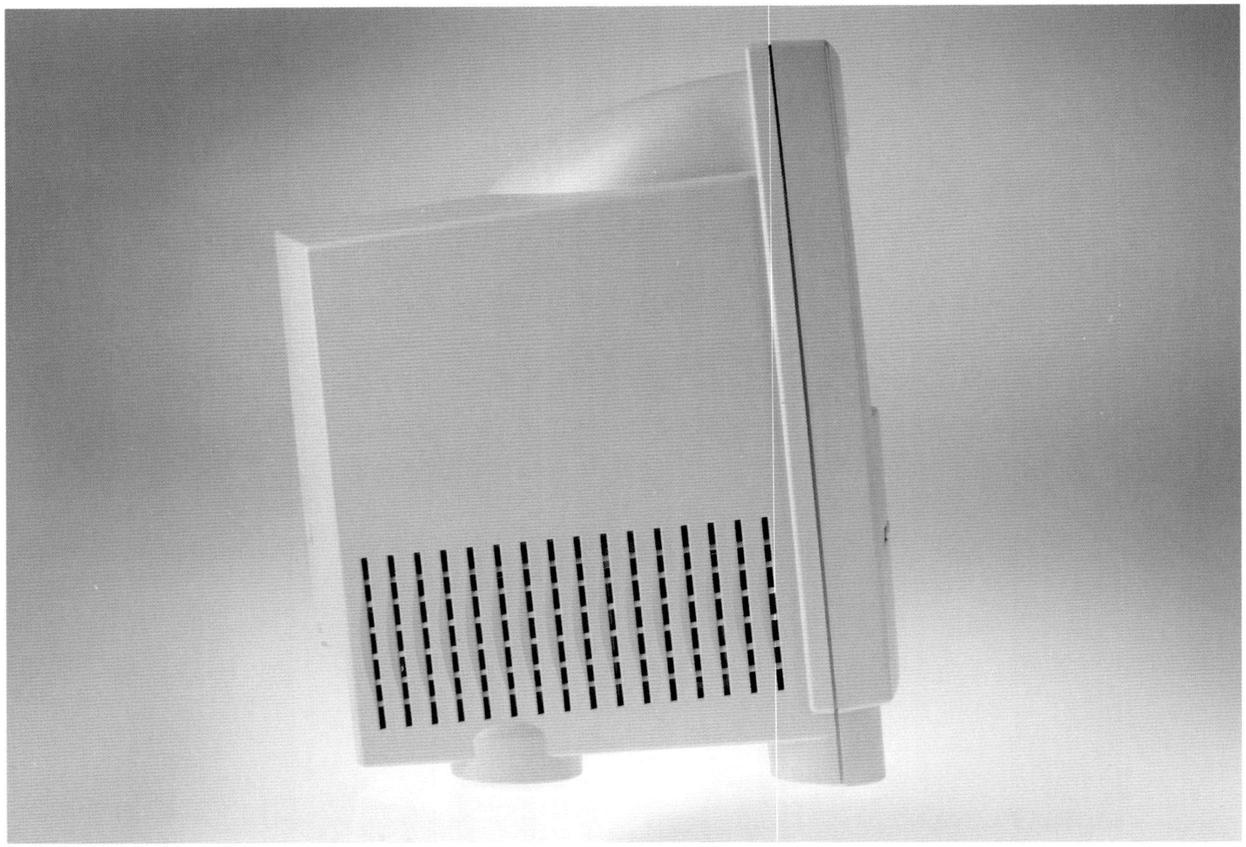

◂ Macintosh Color Classic, 1993; Macintosh Quadra 610, 1993 ▸

DOS Compatible

"Apple has always created products to connect with people. It was always to empower people that we created products. Some companies wanted to create great hardware . . . our goal has always been to empower people, to connect with people." —Bill Fernandez

▲ Macintosh Quadra 950, 1992 ▸

Macintosh
Quadra 950

"I loved my first Macintosh. It felt like the most special and incredible object I had ever seen and owned. I dreamed of a day when I could have color, or maybe even moving images—and that day came a few years later when I helped to create QuickTime, advancing the Macintosh again with a delightful quantum leap that changed personal computing forever." —**Eric Hoffert, Co-founder of Apple QuickTime**

Power Macintosh 7200, 1995 ▸

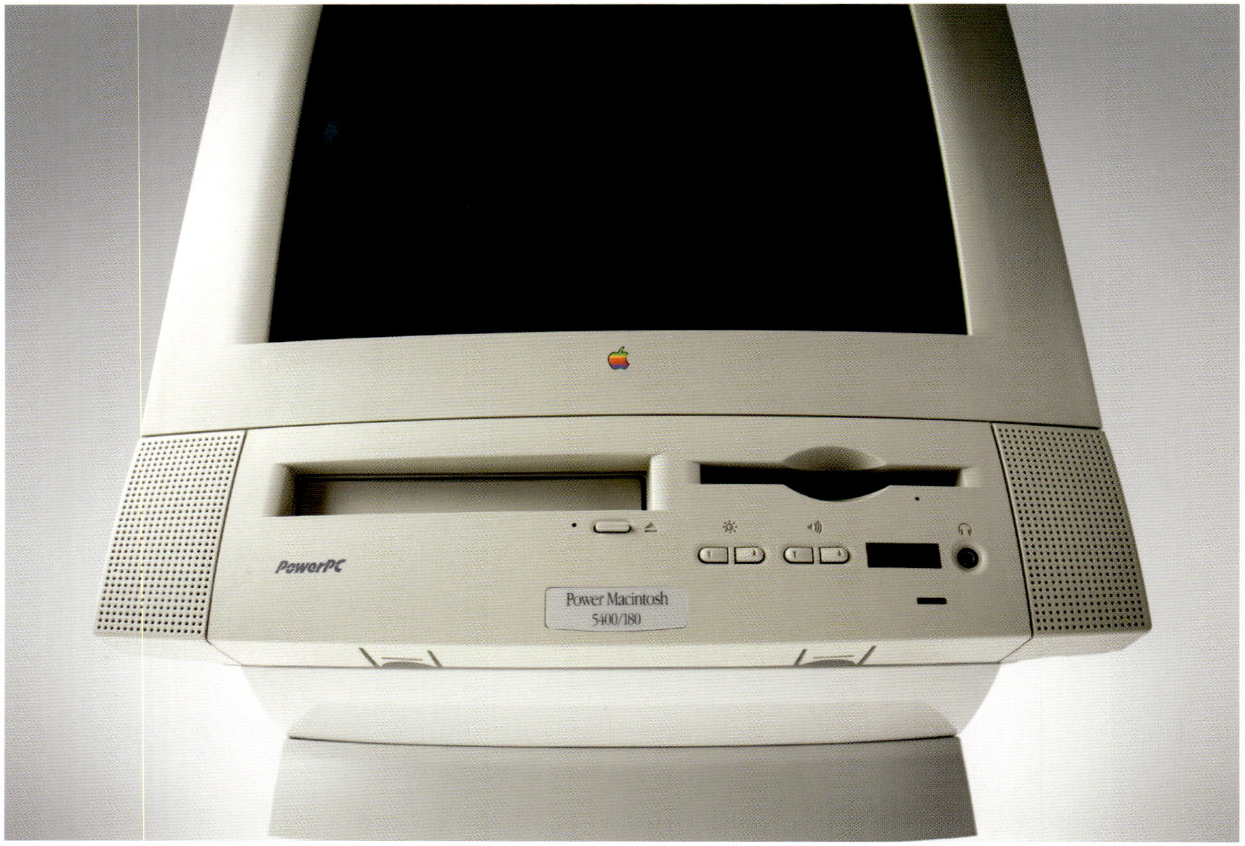

Power Macintosh 5400, 1996 ▸

Power Macintosh
7200/120 PC Compatible

◂ Apple Network Server, 1996 ▸

"You have to deeply understand the essence of a product in order to be able to get rid of the parts that are not essential."

—Jonathan Ive, Senior Vice President of Industrial Design, Apple Inc.

◂ iMac G3, 1998

◂ iMac G3 "Flower Power," 2001

iMac G3, 1998 ▸

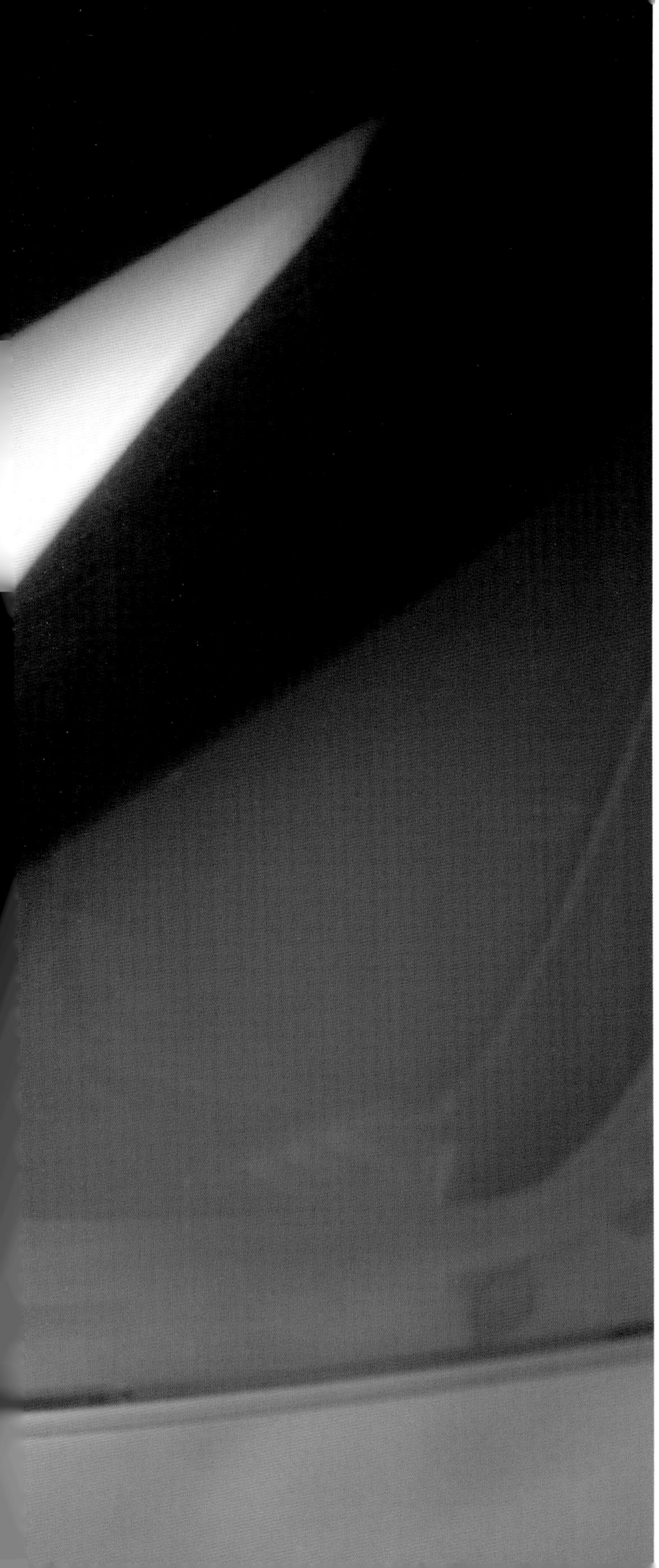

"Seeing an object with a handle, you instantly understand aspects of its physical nature—I can touch it, move it, it's not too precious."

—Jonathan Ive

◂ iMac G3/400 DV SE Graphite, 1999

"The experience you create is the real goal of selling these technology products. ...And if you want to be successful, you have to create an experience that makes people happy and makes them want to buy your product ...Well that's always been implicit with the Apple way, even though we didn't really know what to call it in those days."

—Bill Fernandez

▼ eMac, 2002 ▶

▼ Macintosh TV, 1993

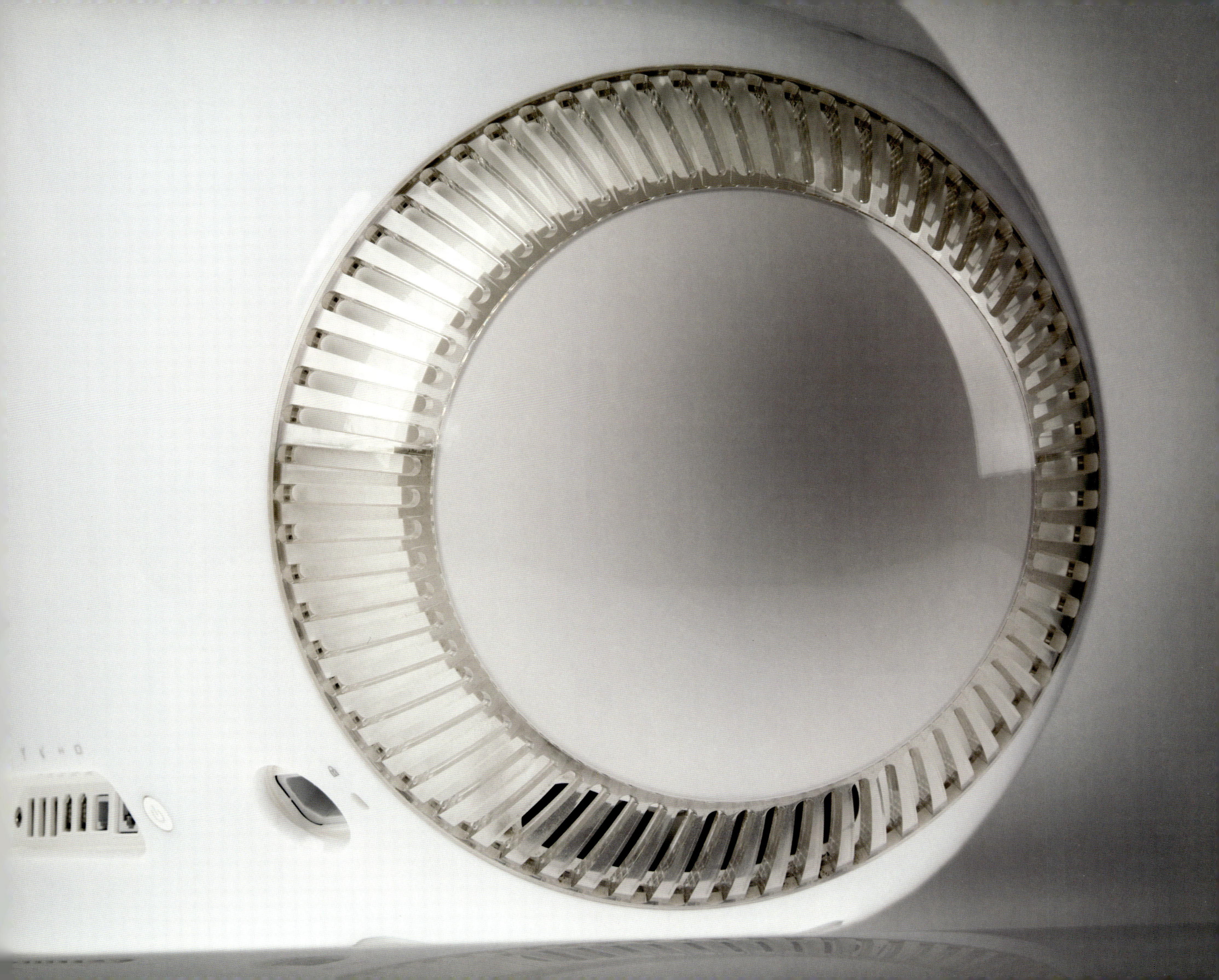

"A computer absolutely can be sexy."

—Jonathan Ive

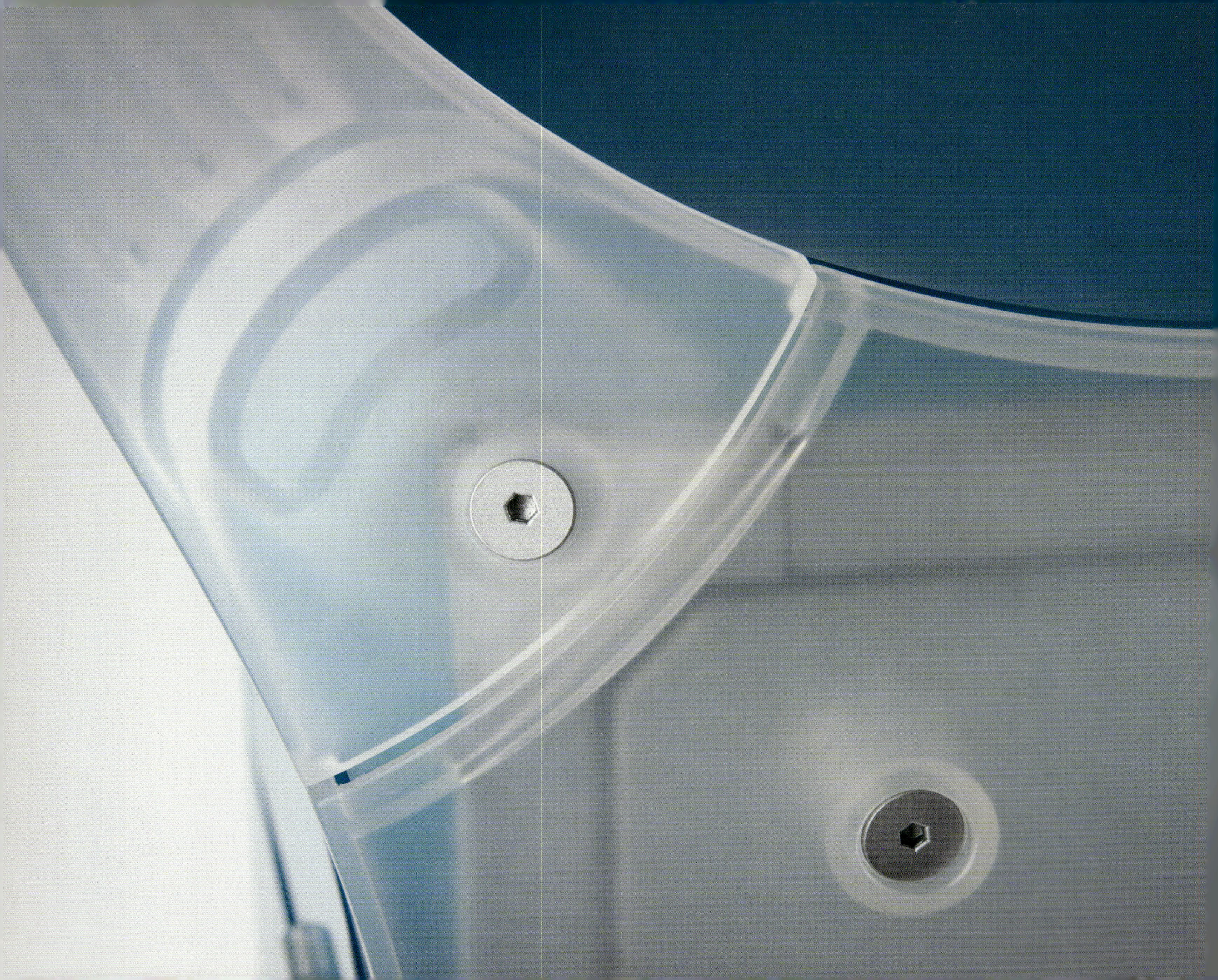

"These have to be objects that are totally seductive."

—Jonathan Ive

◂ ◂ Power Macintosh G3, 1999 ▸

"You don't often get to design something out of one piece of plastic. This was about simplifying, removing clutter, not just visual but audio clutter. That's why the core is suspended in air."

—Jonathan Ive

◂ Power Mac G4 Cube, 2000 ▸

"At some level, I think you're aware of a calm and considered solution that therefore speaks about how you're going to use it—not the terrible struggles that we as designers and engineers had in trying to solve some of the problems. That's quite obsessive isn't it?" —Jonathan Ive

◂ Power Mac G4 Cube, 2000 ▾

"Simplicity is not the absence of clutter, that's a consequence of simplicity. Simplicity is somehow essentially describing the purpose and place of an object and product. The absence of clutter is just a clutter-free product. That's not simple." —Jonathan Ive

◂ Mac mini Server, 2005; Mac mini Server, 2010 ▸

"The most important thing to Apple is to make the best products in the world that enrich customers' lives. That's our high order bit." —Tim Cook, CEO, Apple Inc.

iMac G4, 2002 ▸

"And then we had our big idea ... Why don't we let each element be true to itself. If the screen's flat, let it be flat. If the computer wants to be horizontal, let it be horizontal ... a beauty and a grace that is gonna last the next decade."

—**Steve Jobs**

◂ iMac G4, 2002 ▸

"It's sad and frustrating that we are surrounded by products that seem to testify to a complete lack of care. That's an interesting thing about an object. One object speaks volumes about the company that produced it and its values and priorities." —Jonathan Ive

◂ "Quicksilver" Power Macintosh G4, 2001 ▸

"I think more significant, more exciting is the indication—is the signal that Apple takes design very seriously—that Apple is prepared to innovate, maybe ask more questions than provide answers for, but that we're pushing design extremely aggressively as we close the millennium."

—Jonathan Ive, 1997

◂ Twentieth Anniversary Macintosh, 1997 ▸

"So if you imagine an object that is a television, that's a radio, that's a computer . . . you imagine all of those functionalities, all of those technologies. You imagine them converging into one object. What should that object be? What on earth should it look like?"

—Jonathan Ive, launch of the Twentieth Anniversary Macintosh, 1997

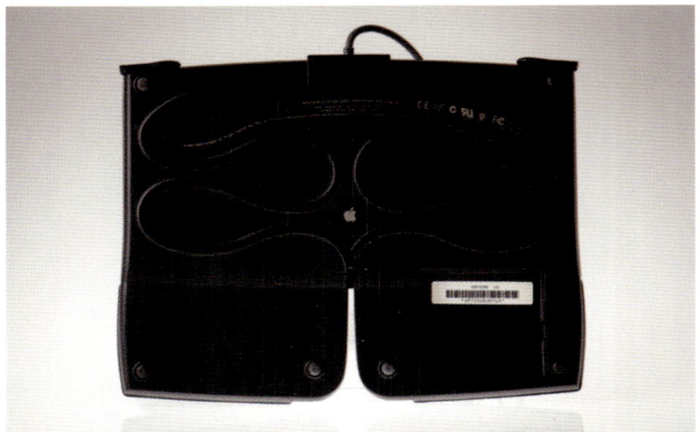

◂ Twentieth Anniversary Macintosh (keyboard), 1997 ▸
Power Macintosh G3 AIO (All-in-One), 1998 ▸ ▸

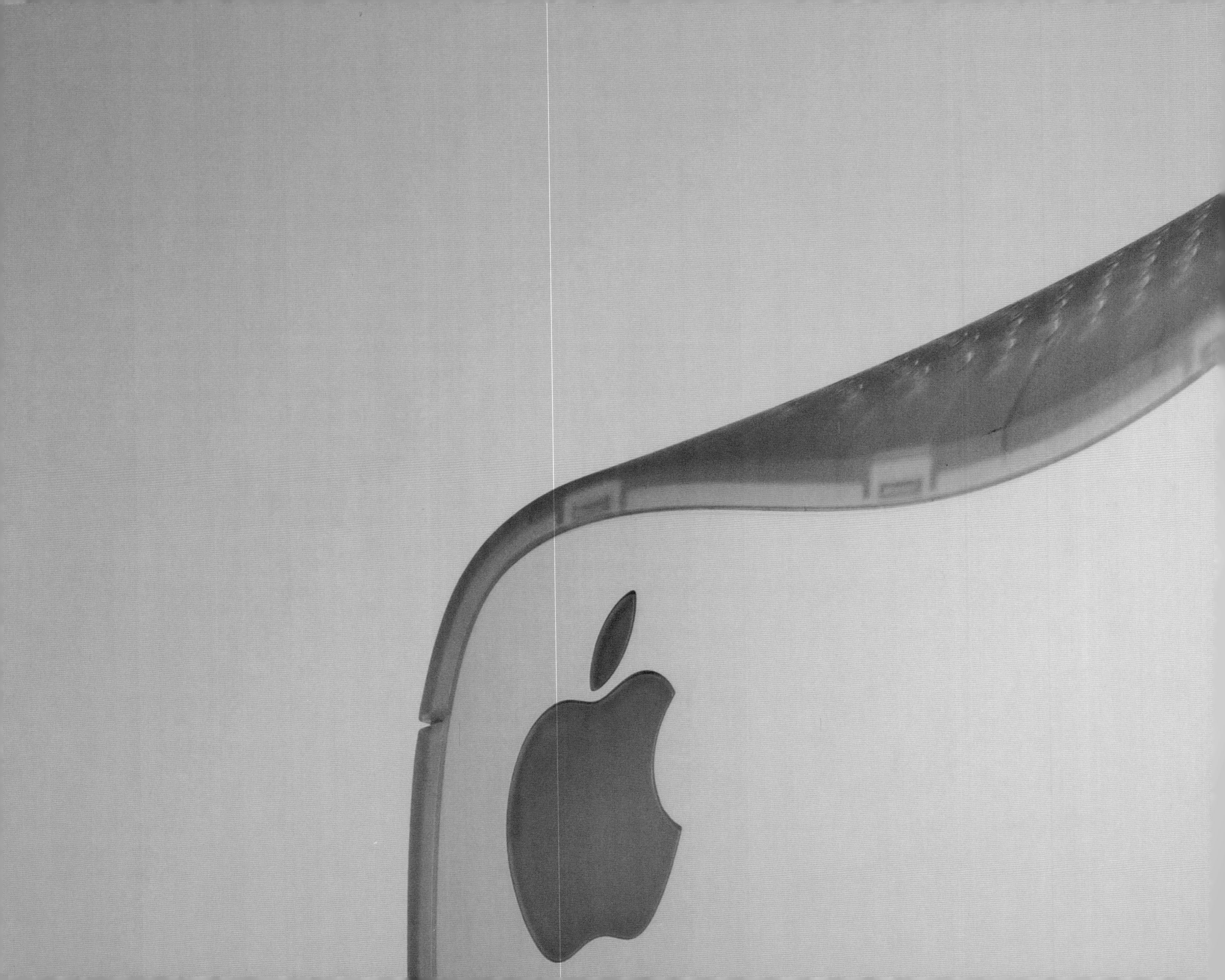

"...Simplicity, elegance, beauty, cleverness, humility. Directness. Truth. Zoom out enough and you can see that the same things that define Apple's products apply to Apple as a whole."

—John Gruber, *Daring Fireball*

◂ ◂ Mac Pro, 2011 ▸ ▸

in
optical
audio
out

"There's no way to look at anything built by Apple and not see the simple elegance that they have captured as their brand."

—Kelli Richards, former director of music and entertainment markets, Apple Inc.

◂ iMac G5, 2004 ▸

"Today you find only a few companies that take design seriously, as I see it. And at the moment, that is an American company. It is Apple."

—Dieter Rams, industrial designer

◂ iMac, 2008 ▾ ▸

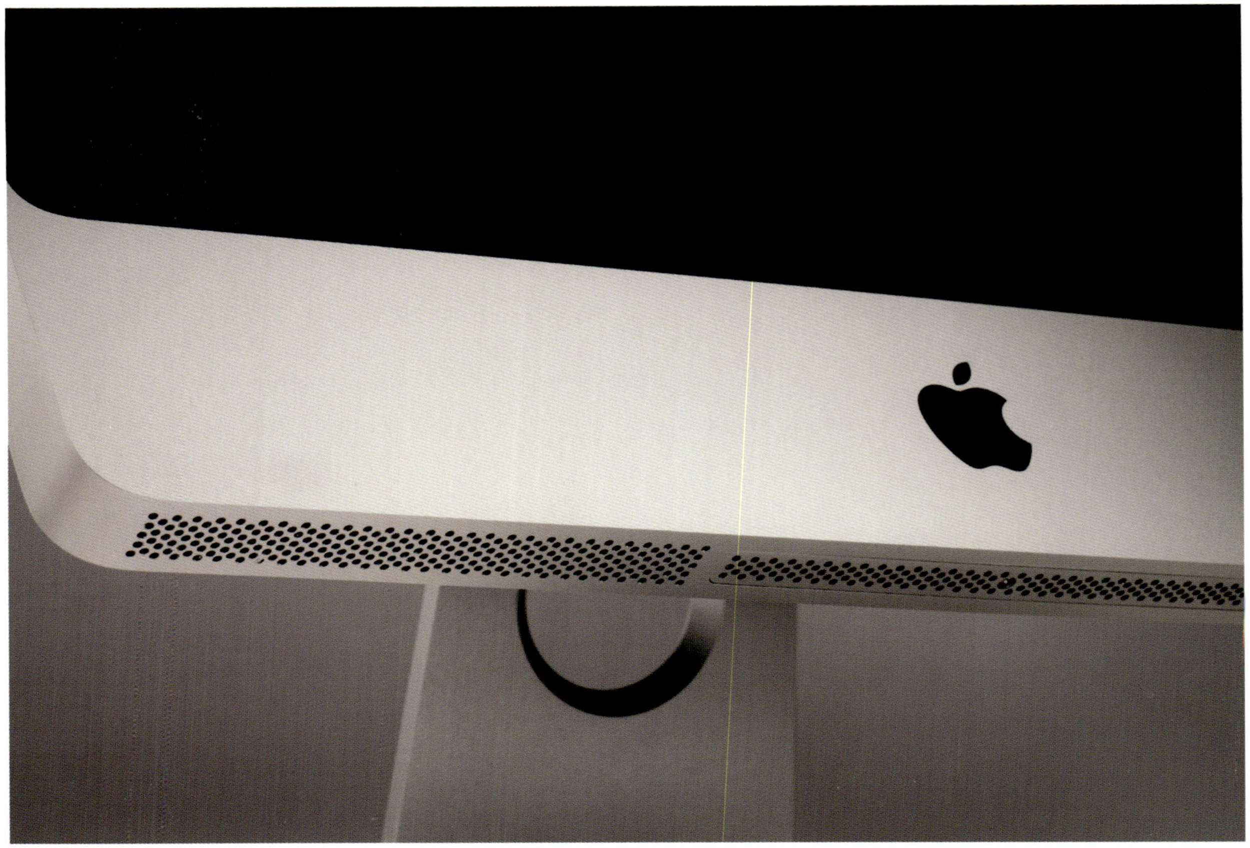

"It's called plasma deposition, and it involves coating the glass with layers of silicon dioxide and niobium pentoxide so precise and so thin they're measured in atoms." —**Apple marketing material, launch of 2012 iMac**

◂ ▾ iMac, 2012

"We're going to make a great product. That's the only religion that we have. We must do something great, something bold, something ambitious."

—Tim Cook

◂ ▾ iMac, 2012 ▸

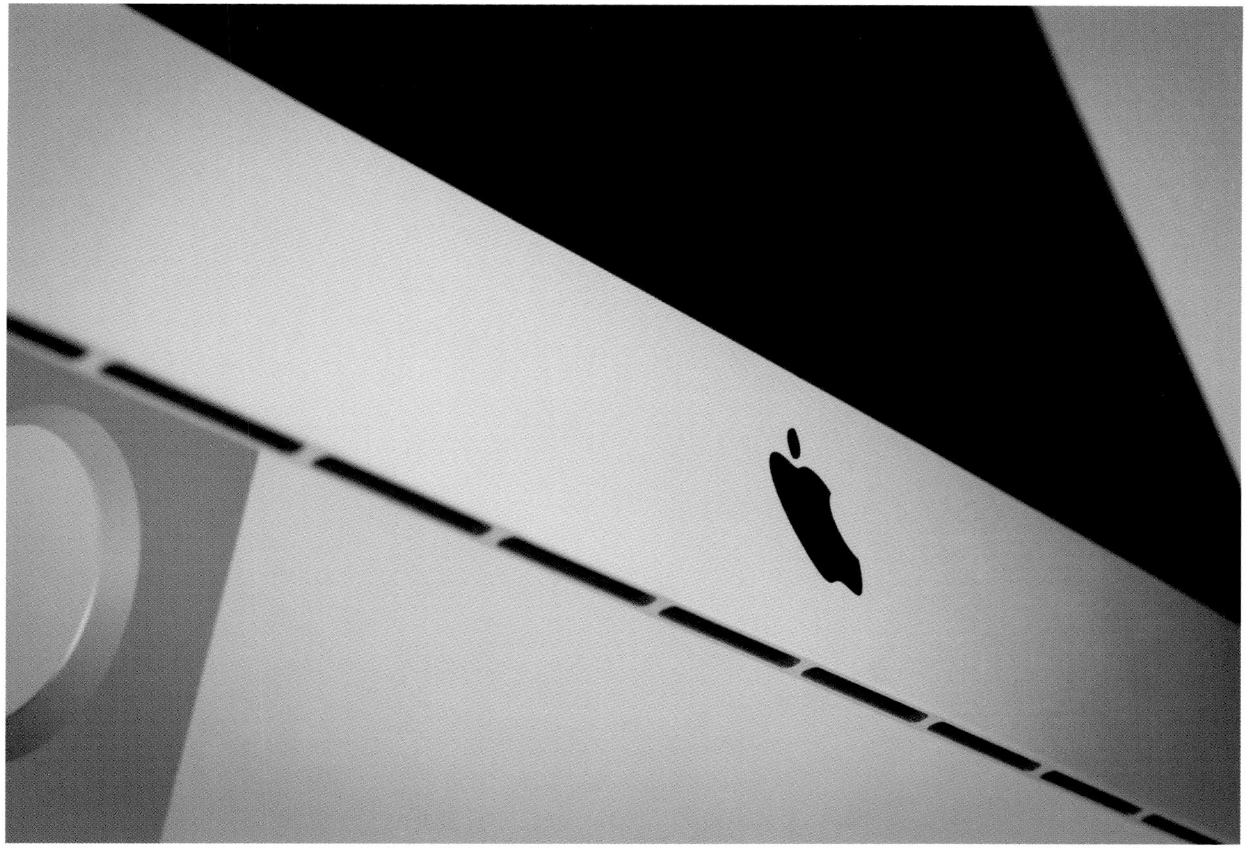

Ken Segall, *creative director, author of* Insanely Simple

I remember the day in 1989 when several of us from Apple's ad agency were invited to witness history. In a conference room inside one of the funky buildings on Bandley Drive, we were to witness the start of a new era. Macintosh was going mobile.

This was our first glimpse of the Macintosh Portable, the first Mac you could take anywhere—assuming you had the muscle to haul its sixteen pounds' worth of heft.

Two years later came the PowerBooks. An inch-and-a-half thick, they were clunky by today's standards, but wow, did I love my PowerBook 140. I couldn't wait to show it off to friends. With the built-in trackball, you didn't even need a mouse anymore. How cool was that?

All of these advances happened on John Sculley's watch. When Steve Jobs returned to Apple and hooked up with Jonathan Ive, the laptop got sexier. With its gorgeous black curves, the PowerBook G3 was, as we called it in ads, "a Formula One race car in an Armani suit." After that came the titanium PowerBook, which fairly quickly led to a more timeless aluminum.

Riffing off the iMac design, Ive delivered a laptop designed for home users: iBook. It's tough to look at by today's standards, coming in a choice of gaudy blue or orange, sporting a handle that made manly men look like they were carrying a purse. But iBook had magic on its side. Steve got up on stage and revealed the first mainstream computer that could actually connect to the Internet without wires. Imagine that.

It's interesting to note that at every point in the evolution of the laptop, Apple innovations have been the catalyst for the PC industry. From the trackball to the trackpad, from wi-fi to ultra-thin computers, Apple has thrived on blazing new trails—creating computers that are a unique blend of design and functionality.

PORTABLES

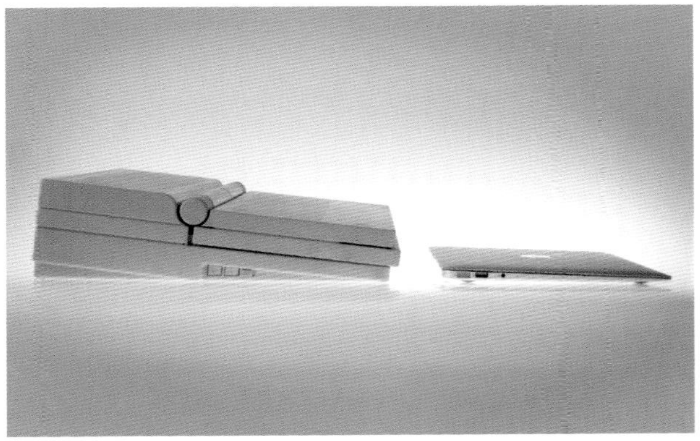

Macintosh Portable

"When we set out to design the Macintosh Portable, we had three sets of challenges in mind—portability, consistency, and battery paranoia, and we wanted absolutely no compromise in dealing with these challenges."

—Jean-Louis Gassée, former president, Apple Inc.,
launch of the Macintosh Portable, 1989

◂ Macintosh Portable, 1989 ▾

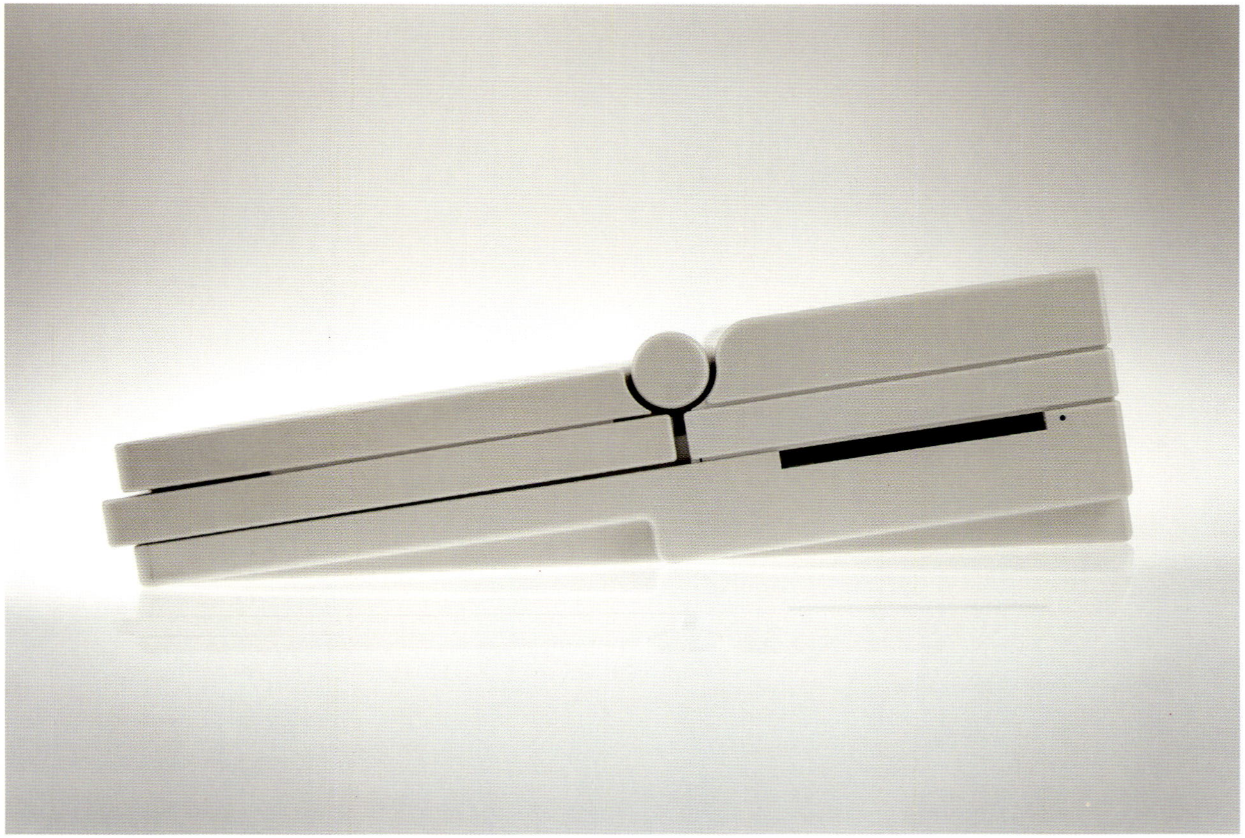

Macintosh PowerBook 100, 1991 ▸

K
M
enter

"We want ideas coming from all of our 80,000 people, not five or three."

—Tim Cook

◂ ▾ Macintosh PowerBook 170 LPGA Special Edition, 1992 ▸

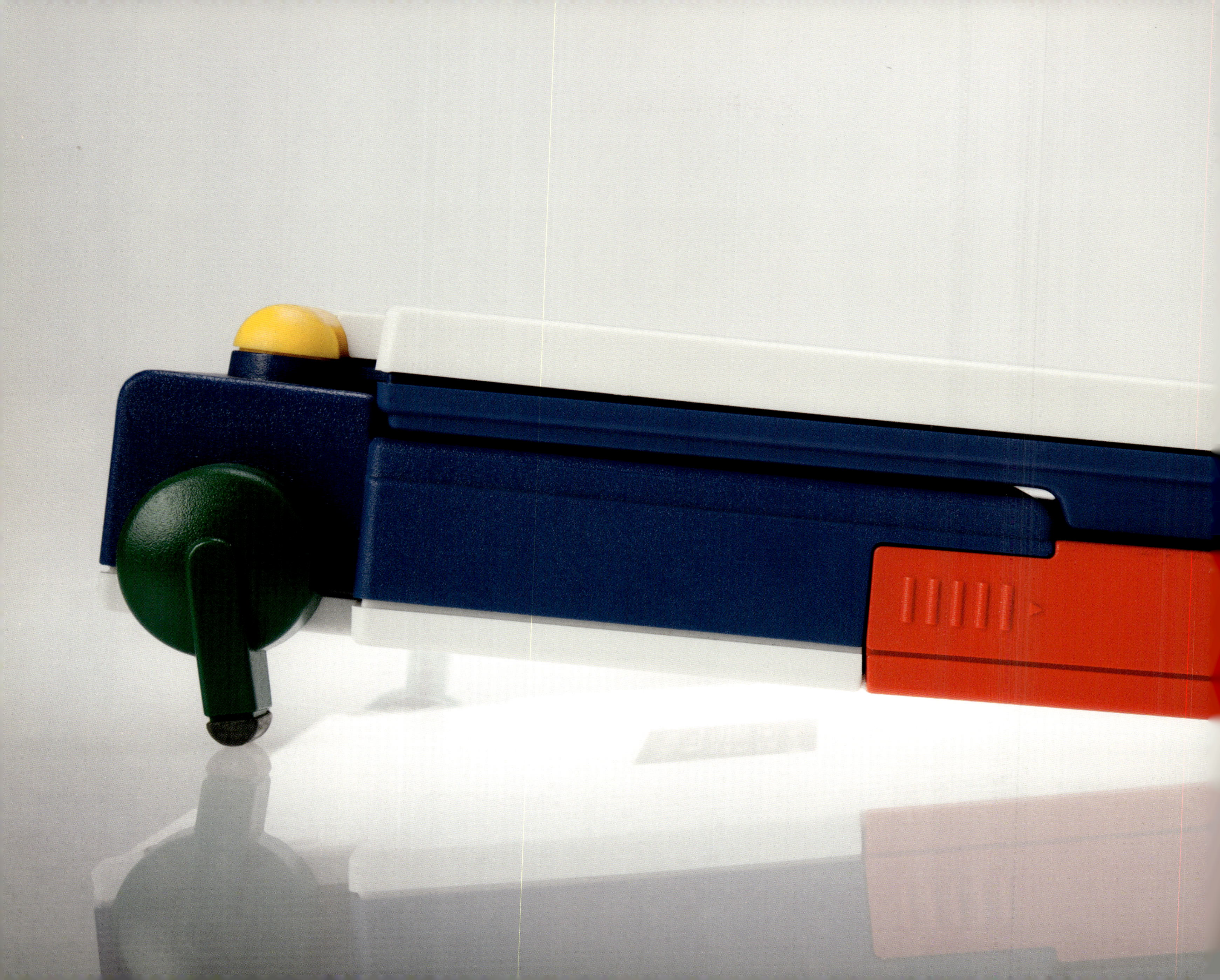

◂ Macintosh PowerBook 170 LPGA Special Edition, 1992; Macintosh PowerBook 150, 1994 ▾

"It's really important in a product to have a sense of the hierarchy of what's important and what's not important by removing those things that are vying for your attention." —Jonathan Ive

◂ Macintosh PowerBook 150, 1994

Macintosh PowerBook Duo 2300c and Duo MiniDock, 1995 ▸

◂ Macintosh PowerBook Duo 2300c and Dock II, 1995 ▸

eject

PowerBook 550c

◂ Macintosh PowerBook 550c, 1995 ▾

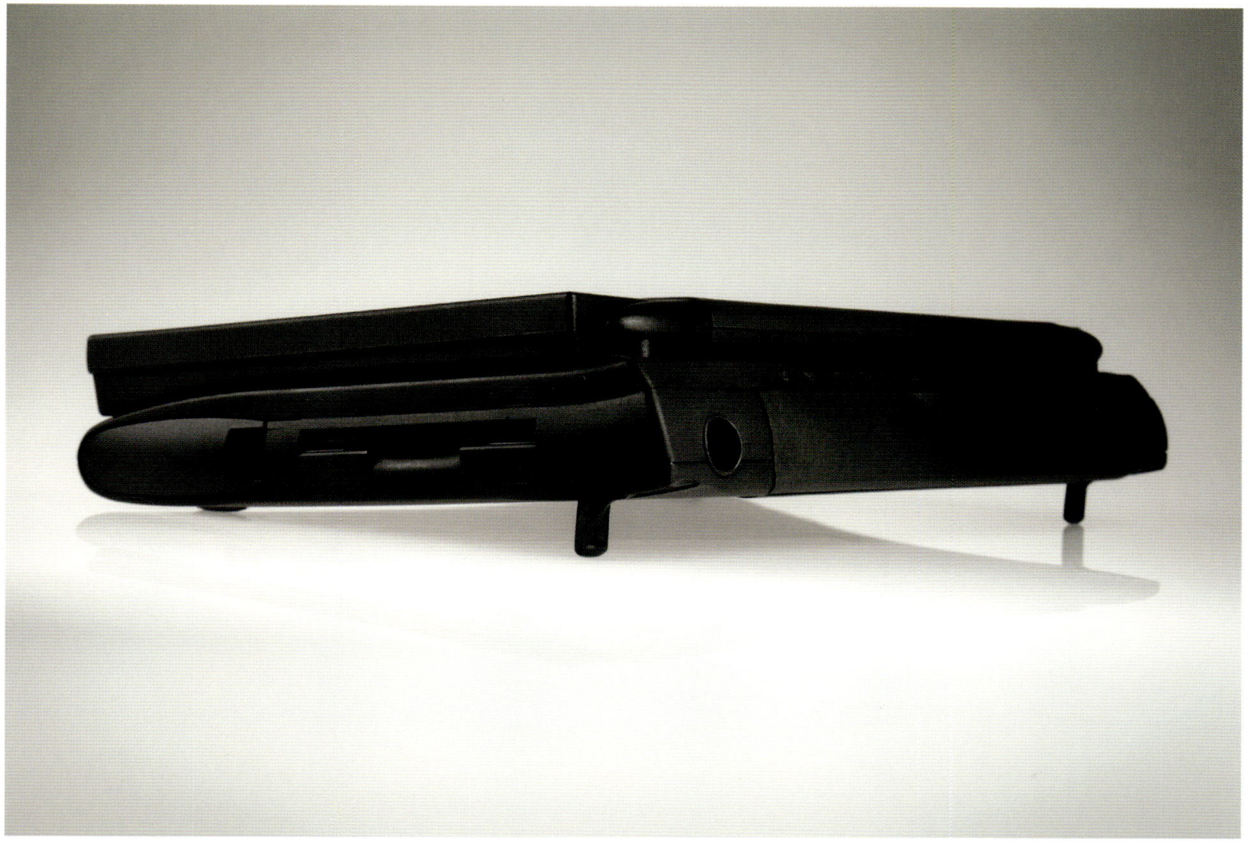

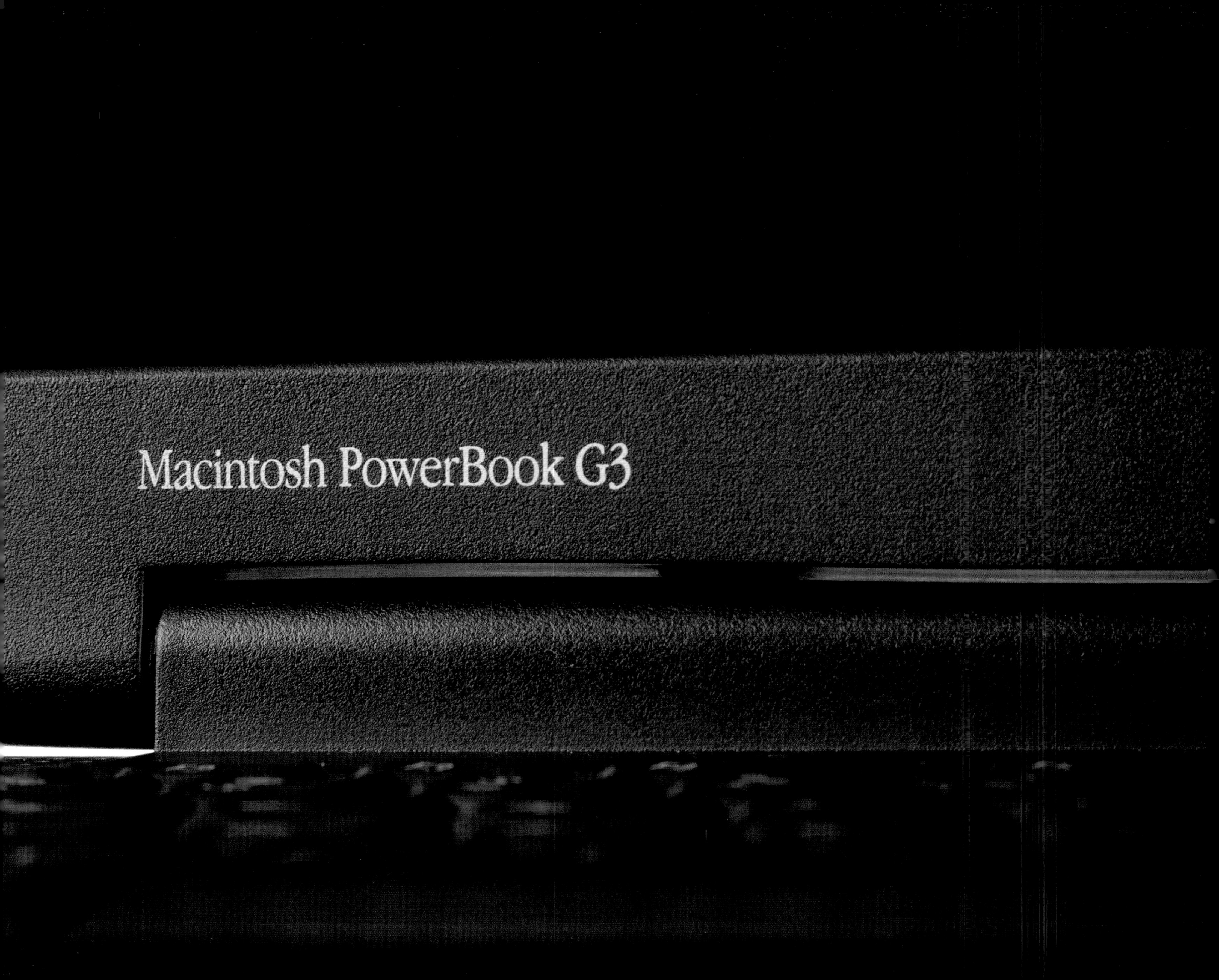
Macintosh PowerBook G3

enter

"Clearly, if Vannevar Bush had lived to be a hundred and two, he would have bought a PowerBook."

—Steven Levy, author of *Insanely Great*

◂ Macintosh PowerBook G3 Series, 1998

◂ Macintosh PowerBook G3, 1997 ▸

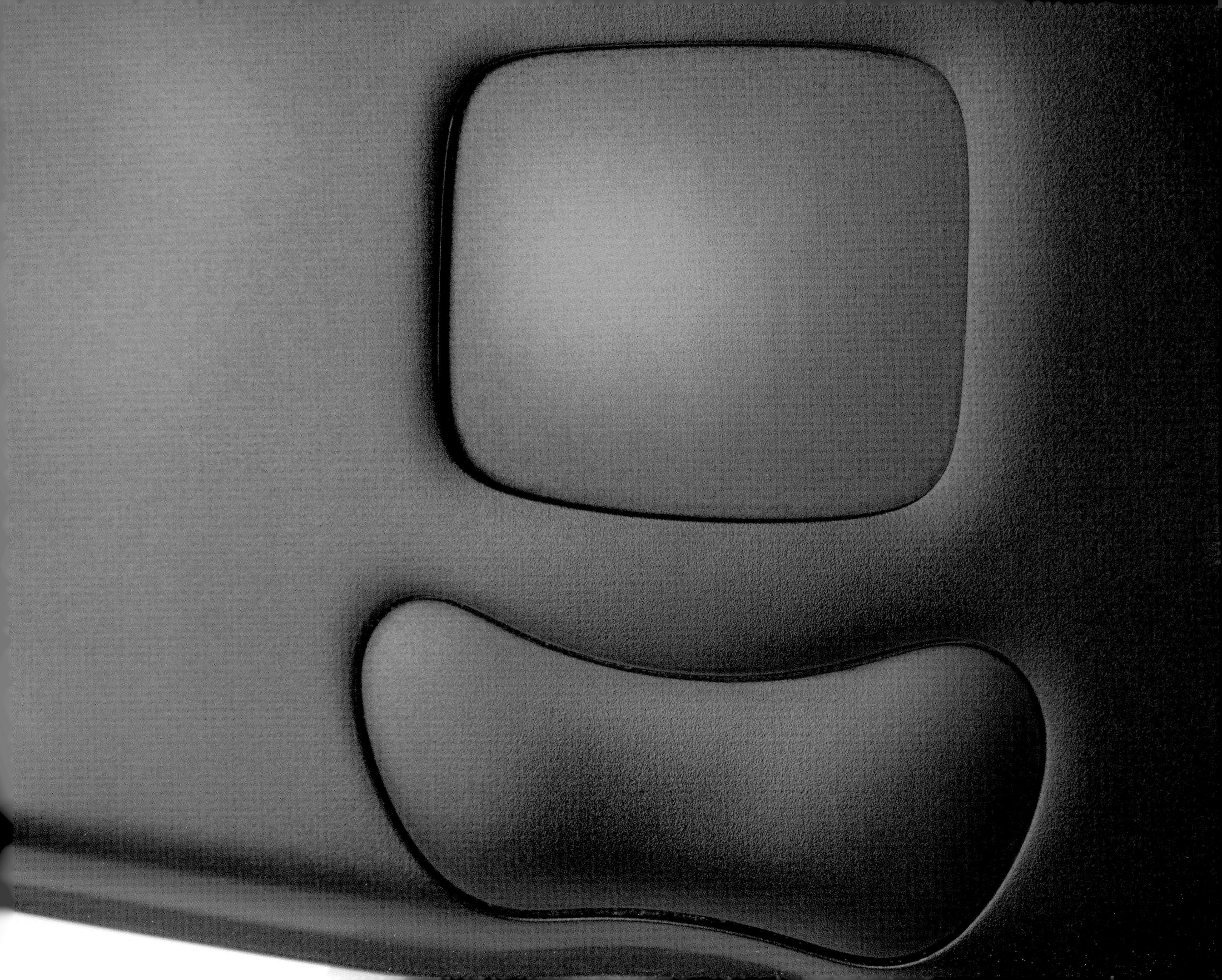

"We're trying to design simple happy shapes—you know shapes that when you look at them it's sort of tough not to smile." —Jonathan Ive

iBook G3 "Clamshell" (Graphite), 2000 ►
◄ iBook G3 "Clamshell" (Lime), 2000 ► ►

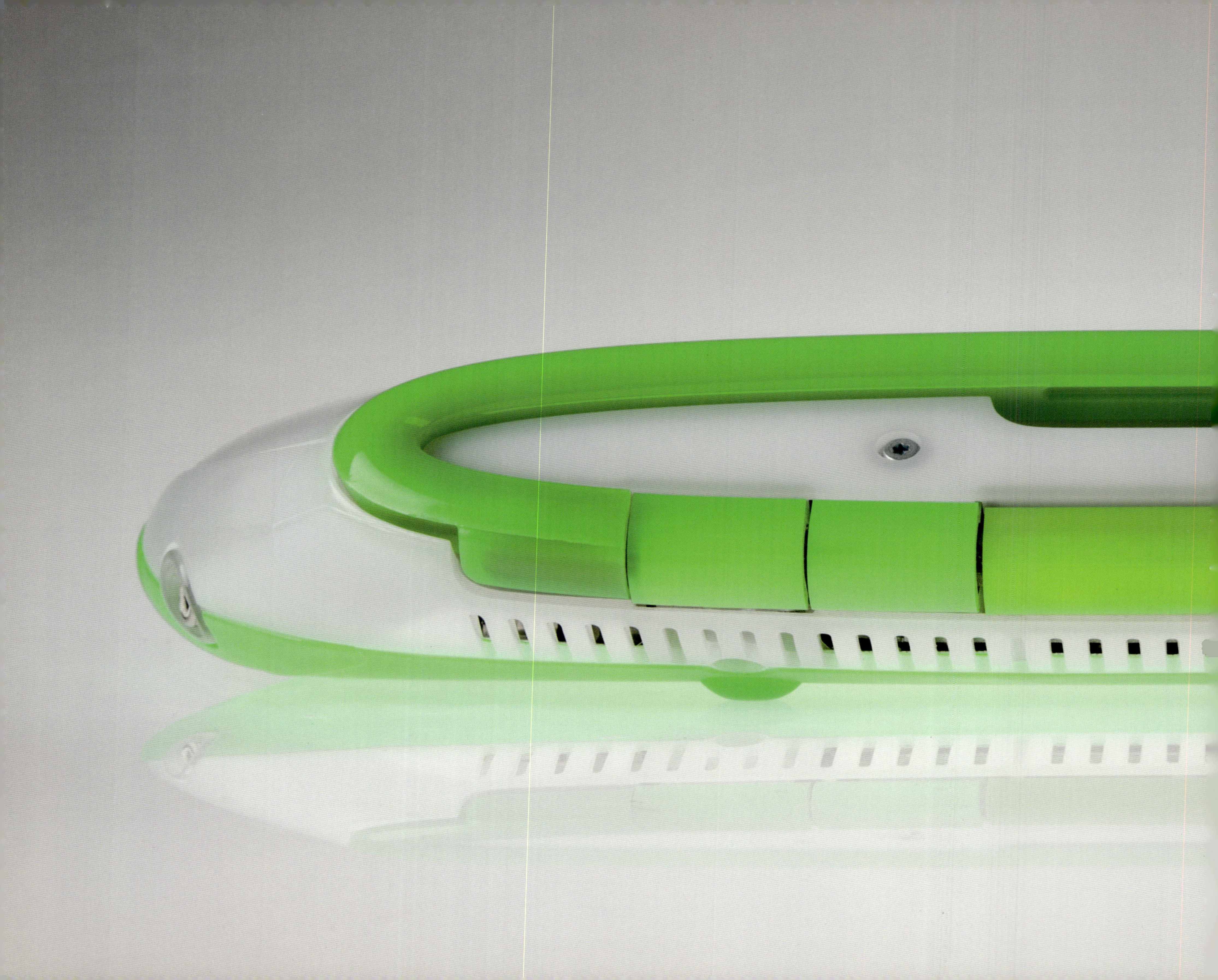

esc
F1
F2
F3
F4
~
`
!
1
@
2
#
3
$
4
%
5
tab
Q
W
E
R

◂ iBook G3 "Clamshell" (Tangerine), 2000

"This is polycarbonate plastic—this is the stuff they make bulletproof vests out of."

—Steve Jobs, launch of iBook

▴ ◂ iBook G3 "Clamshell" (Lime), 2000

F8
F9
F10
F11
F12
9
0

"The memory of how we work will endure beyond the products of our work."

—Jonathan Ive

◂ iBook G4 "Snow," 2001

W
E
R
S
D
F
Z
X
C

◂ Macintosh PowerBook G4, 2005 ▾

"I remember the first time I saw an Apple product. I remember it so clearly… I got a very clear sense of the people that designed it and made it."

—Jonathan Ive

◂ Macintosh PowerBook G4, 2001 ▸

PowerBook G4

D
C
S
X
Z
alt
option
comm

"Our role is to imagine products that don't exist and guide them to life."

—Christopher Stringer, Industrial Designer, Apple Inc.

◂ ◂ MacBook, 2006 ▸

"When we're presented with an object that is complex, it can be intimidating. It certainly can give you the sense that we don't understand it. And we are often intimidated, aren't we, by objects and products that we don't understand. So clarity and simplicity are, I think, critically important for us to be able to understand a product and enjoy using it."

—Jonathan Ive

◂ MacBook, 2006 ▸

"Apple does a great job of creating these objects of lust—

You just want to have it, you just want to touch it, play with it."

—Ken Segall, former creative director for Apple Inc.,
author of *Insanely Simple*

◂ MacBook, 2006

"If you never change anything, then what you can really engineer is kind of incremental. But when you're willing to change things, then you kind of open up a whole new world of design."

—Bob Mansfield, Senior Vice President of Technologies, Apple Inc., launch of 2012 MacBook Pro

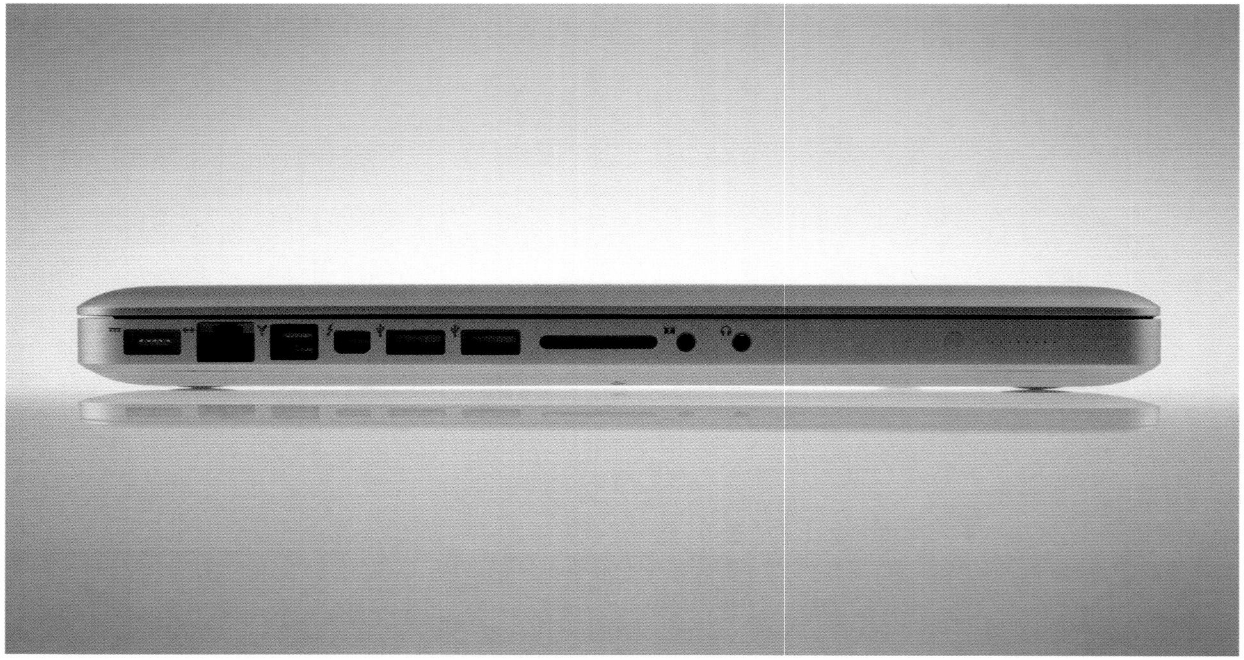

◂ MacBook Pro, 2009 ▸

"The thickest part of the MacBook Air is still thinner than the thinnest part of the [Sony] TZ series. We're talking thin here."

—Steve Jobs, launch of the MacBook Air

MacBook Air, 2008 ▲

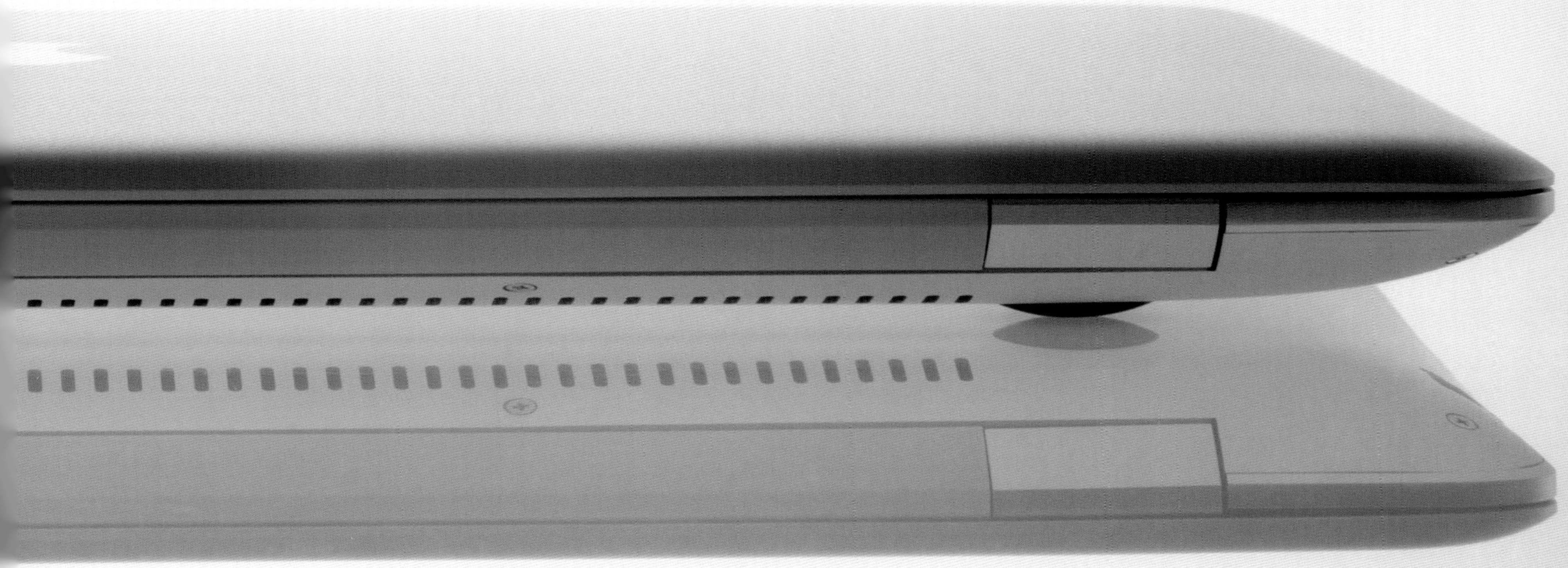

MacBook Air, 2010 ▸

MacBook Air

MacBook Pro, 2012 ▸

James Savage, *Founder and Co-host of* RetroMacCast

The computers and other principal devices Apple has designed throughout its history have received plenty of recognition, and deservedly so. However, if you look beyond them, beside them, or even inside them, you'll see their often-overlooked peripherals. Apple peripherals share a level of quality atypical of the otherwise mundane peripherals available from other manufacturers. For as much thought that goes into the design and engineering of an Apple computer, equal attention is paid to these unheralded peripherals to ensure they are worthy of the Apple logo.

Apple peripherals are physical extensions of the computers to which they are connected, and therefore, their designs are extensions as well. The consistency of design and attention to detail are evident throughout. Examining the evolution of the Apple mouse, which has changed very little in functionality, reveals stark contrasts in design. From the early chamfered-edge, beige mouse to the sleek, minimal lines of the current mouse, each captures the essence of the design language in use at the time.

Likewise, other peripherals like cameras, power supplies, displays, and disk drives are easily associated with their parent computers simply from their materials, shapes and colors.

The extent of Apple's peripheral offerings has varied greatly over the years, peaking during the absence of Steve Jobs. While most of these peripherals did not survive his return and the subsequent refocusing of product lines, some allowed Apple to take risks in new areas or experiment with new design ideas. For example, eMate debuted translucent case plastics long before iMac sported them. Apple's LaserWriter proved instrumental to the success of Macintosh by helping it usher in desktop publishing. Newton introduced the world to the possibilities of mobile computing, paving the way for the PalmPilot and eventually Apple's own iPhone. Apple continues to experiment with peripherals such as the Apple TV. Perhaps history would have been kinder to Newton had it, too, been regarded by Apple as simply a "hobby."

PERIPHERALS

◂ Monochrome Monitor IIe, 1986

IIc Flat Panel Display, 1984 ▸

▲ Monitor IIc, 1984

▲ AudioVision 14" Monitor, 1994

▲ AudioVision 14" Monitor, 1994

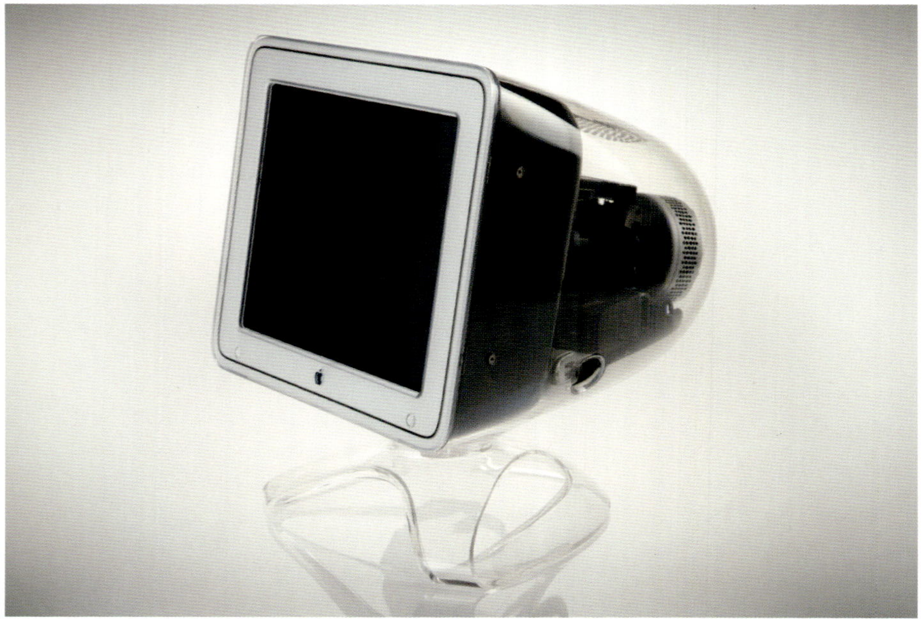

▲ Apple Studio Display 17" CRT, 2000 ►

"We wouldn't do anything that we consider not a great product. It's just not in us to do it, it's not why we're on this earth. There are other companies that do that; that's just not who we are."

—Tim Cook

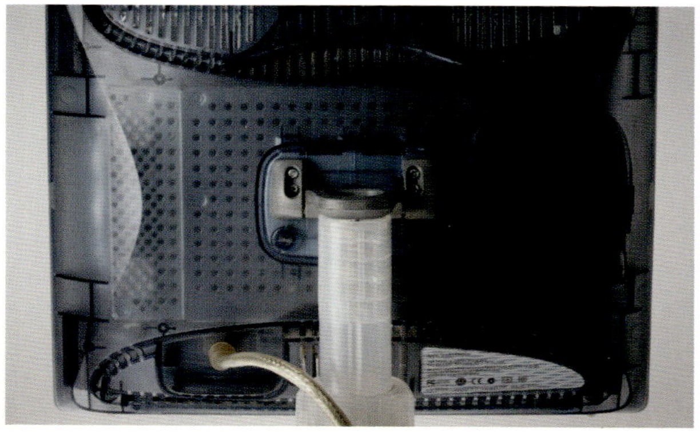

▲ Apple Studio Display, 1999

▼ Apple Studio Display, 2011

Apple Studio Display ,1998 ▸

Apple Studio Display, 2011 ▸

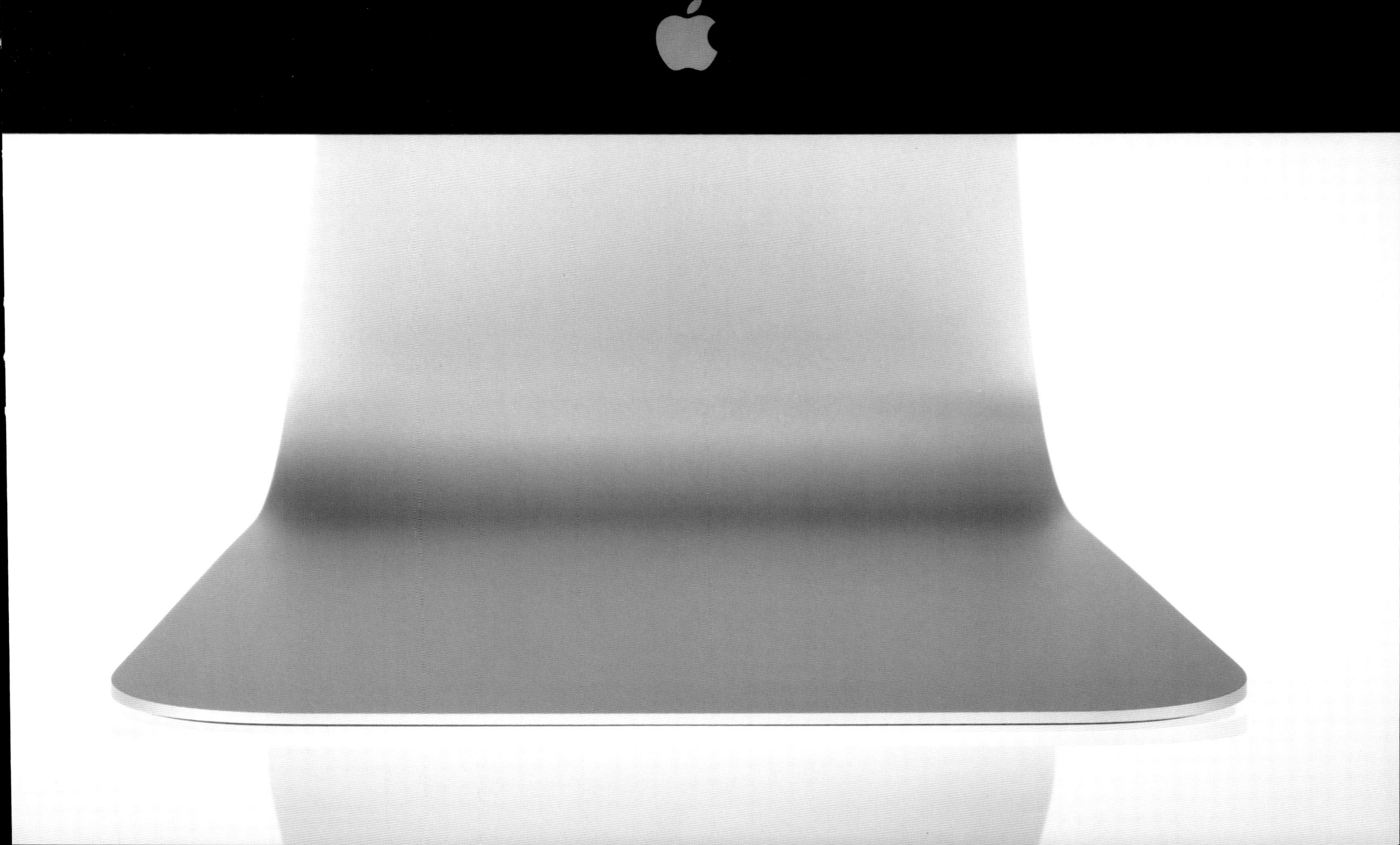

◄ Apple Hand Controllers IIe and IIc

▲ Apple Paddles

▲ Apple Paddles

▲ Apple IIe Joystick

▲ Apple Joystick IIe and IIc

▼ Bandai Pippin, 1995 ► ►

ATMARK TM

◂ Apple TV, 1st Generation, 2007

Apple TV, 3rd Generation, 2012 ▸

tv

"When you first see the mouse, it could not be any simpler. But I love the way that it scales from being something that is apparently simple to actually being really remarkably sophisticated."

—Jonathan Ive, launch of Magic Mouse, 2009

▲ Lisa Mouse, 1983

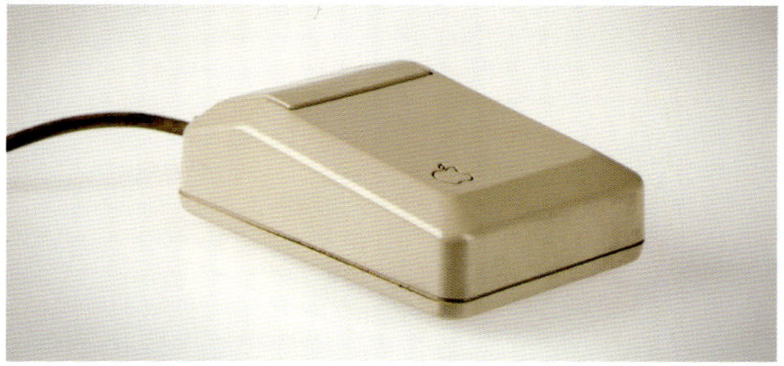

▲ Mouse IIc, 1984

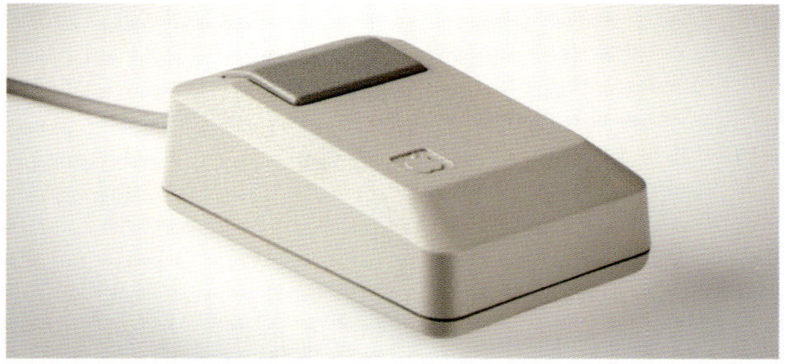

▲ Macintosh Mouse, 1984

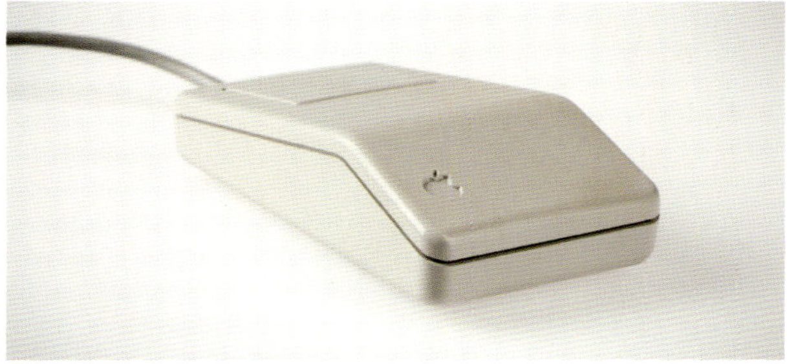

▲ Apple Desktop Bus Mouse, 1986

▲ Apple Desktop Bus Mouse II, 1993

▲ Apple Desktop Bus Mouse II (Black), 1993

▲ USB Mouse, 1998

▲ Pro Mouse (White), 2000

▲ Pro Mouse (Black), 2000

▲ Mighty Mouse, 2005

◄ ▲ Magic Mouse, 2009

▲ Magic Trackpad, 2010

esc
tab
caps lock
shift
control
option
Q W E R T
A S D F G
Z X C V B
Y U I O P
H J K L
N M

"The innovation is so deeply embedded in Apple's culture: the boldness, the ambition, the belief that there aren't limits, the desire among our people to not just make good products but make the very best products in the world, it's as strong as ever, it's deeply embedded, it's in the values, it's in the DNA of the company."

—Tim Cook

◂ Adjustable keyboard, 1993

◂ QuickTake 100, 1994; QuickTake 200, 1996 ▾

QuickTake 100

◂ QuickTake 100, 1994; QuickTake 200, 1996 ▸

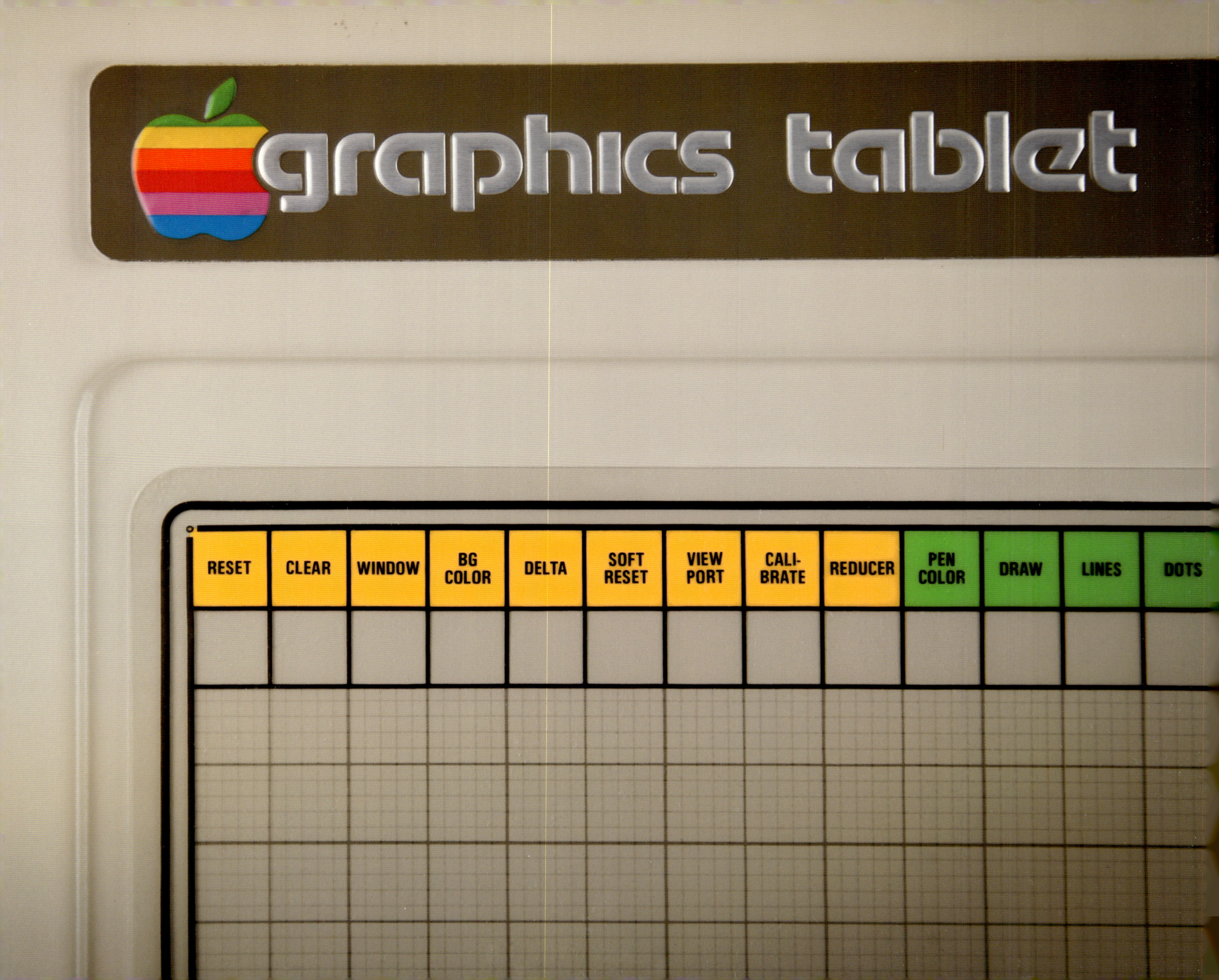
graphics tablet
RESET
CLEAR
WINDOW
BG COLOR
DELTA
SOFT RESET
VIEW PORT
CALI-BRATE
REDUCER
PEN COLOR
DRAW
LINES
DOTS

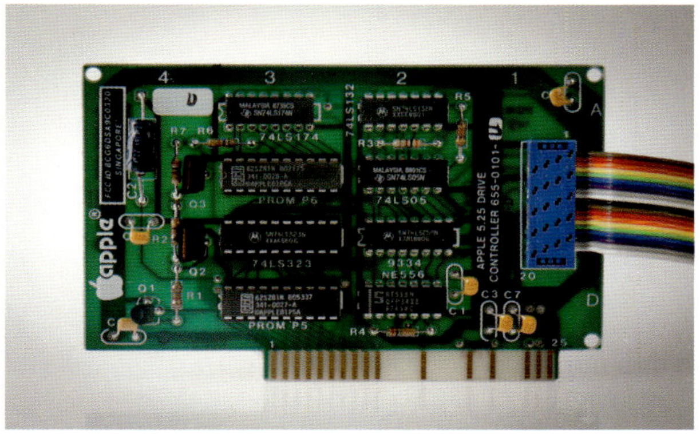

▲ 5.25″ Disk II Controller, 1978

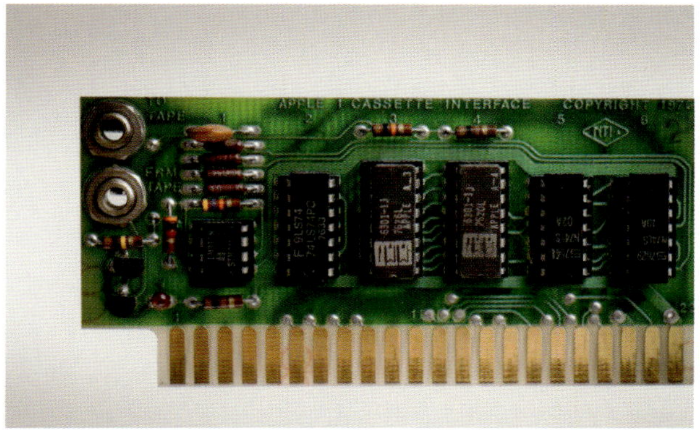

▲ Apple I Cassette Interface, 1976

▲ Ethernet CS II Card, 1996

▲ Apple IIe 80 Column Card, 1981

▲ Apple IIgs Memory Expansion Card, 1986

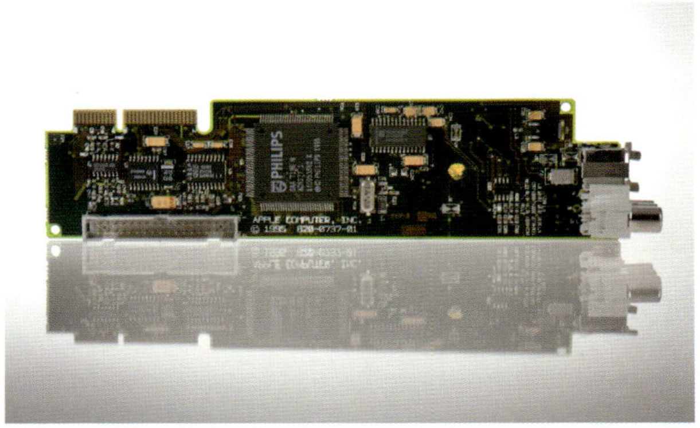

▲ Apple TV/Video System, 1995

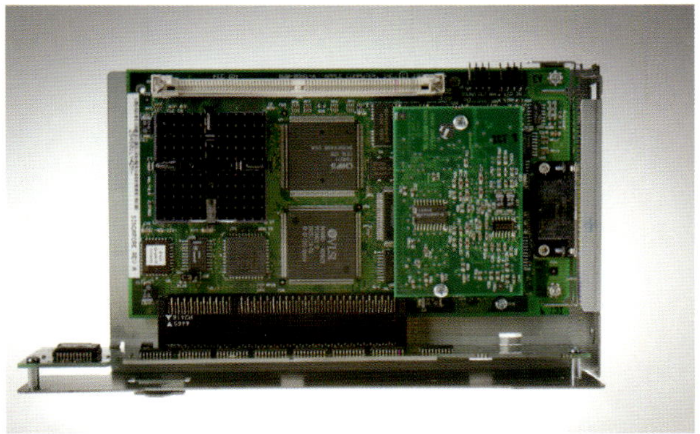

▲ DOS Compatibility Card, 1994

◄ Graphics Tablet, 1979

▲ Imagewriter II 32K Option, 1985

▲ LocalTalk PC Card, 1986

◂ DuoDock II, 1994

Duo MiniDock, 1992 ▸

GeoPort Telecom Adapter Kit, 1993

PowerCD, 1996

◂ Studio Display Power Adapter, 2003

AppleDesign Powered Speakers II, 1994 ▸

AirPort Extreme

"In the 1970s, Apple talked about being at the intersection of technology and the arts. I think that the product qualities are really consequent to the bigger goals that were established when the company was founded. … Caring beyond the functional imperative, we also acknowledge that products have a significance way beyond traditional views of function."

—Jonathan Ive

◂ AirPort Extreme Base Station, 2003

AirPort Extreme Base Station, 2011 ▸

"...The camera is always right on the top of your screen where it needs to be to make that emotional connection with the person on the other end."

—Steve Jobs

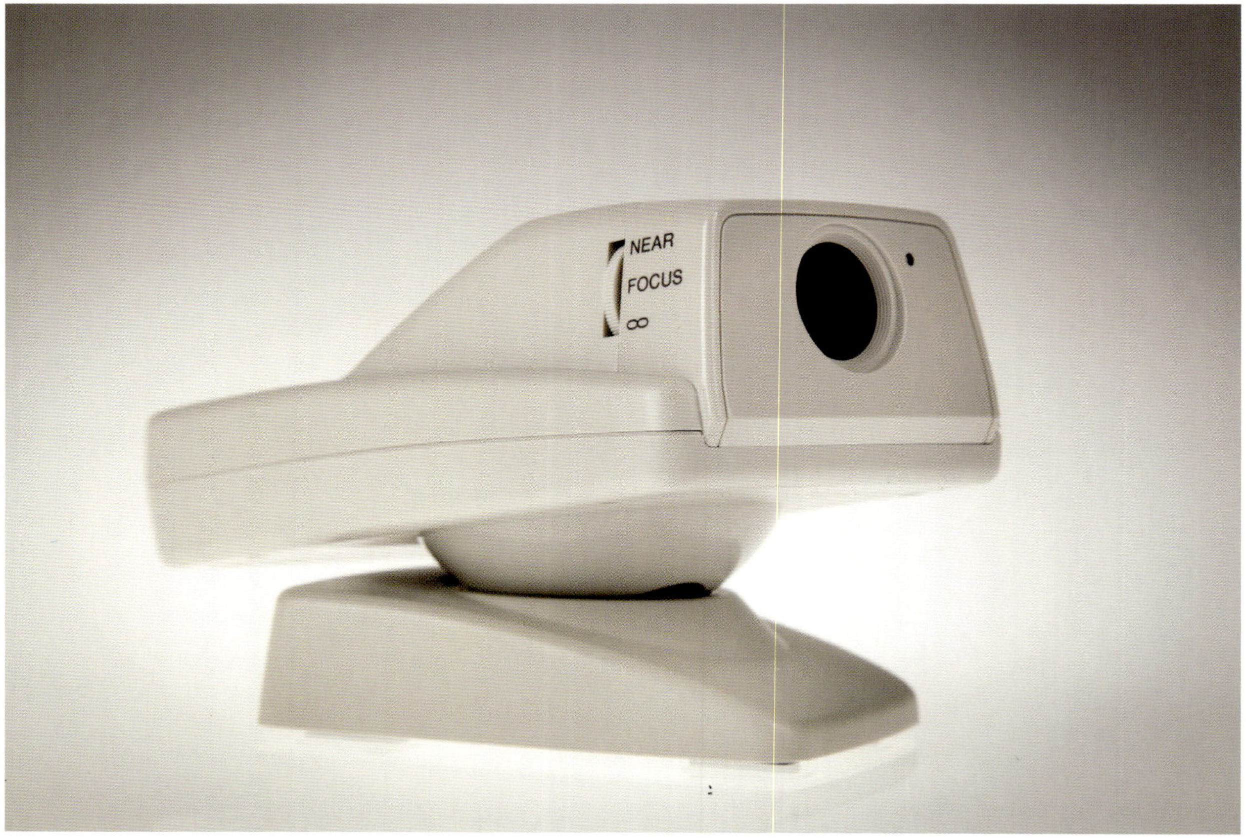

◂ Apple VideoPhone Kit, 1997

"Here's the shutter. Boom. You know, no peeping toms here."

—Steve Jobs, launch of the iSight camera, 2003

iSight, 2003 ▸

"To create something that's genuinely new, you have to start again ... and I think with great intent, you disconnect from the past." —Jonathan Ive

Newton MessagePad 110 Developer Edition, 1994 ▸

Newton MessagePad 100, 1994 ▾

◂ Newton MessagePad 120, 1994 ▾

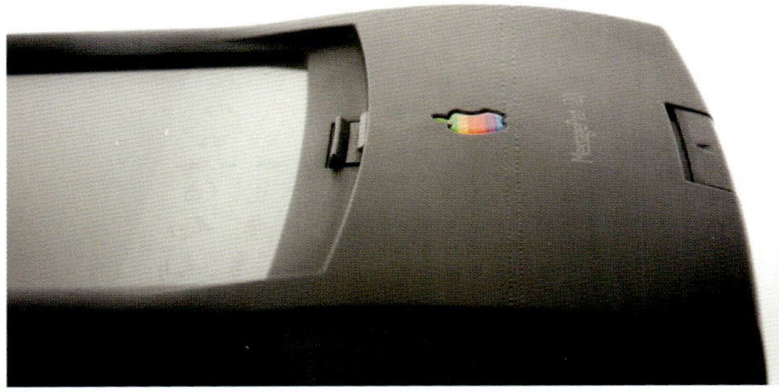

eMate 300
undo
find
assist

◂ eMate 300, 1997

◂ Silentype Printer, 1980

▾ Scribe Printer, 1984

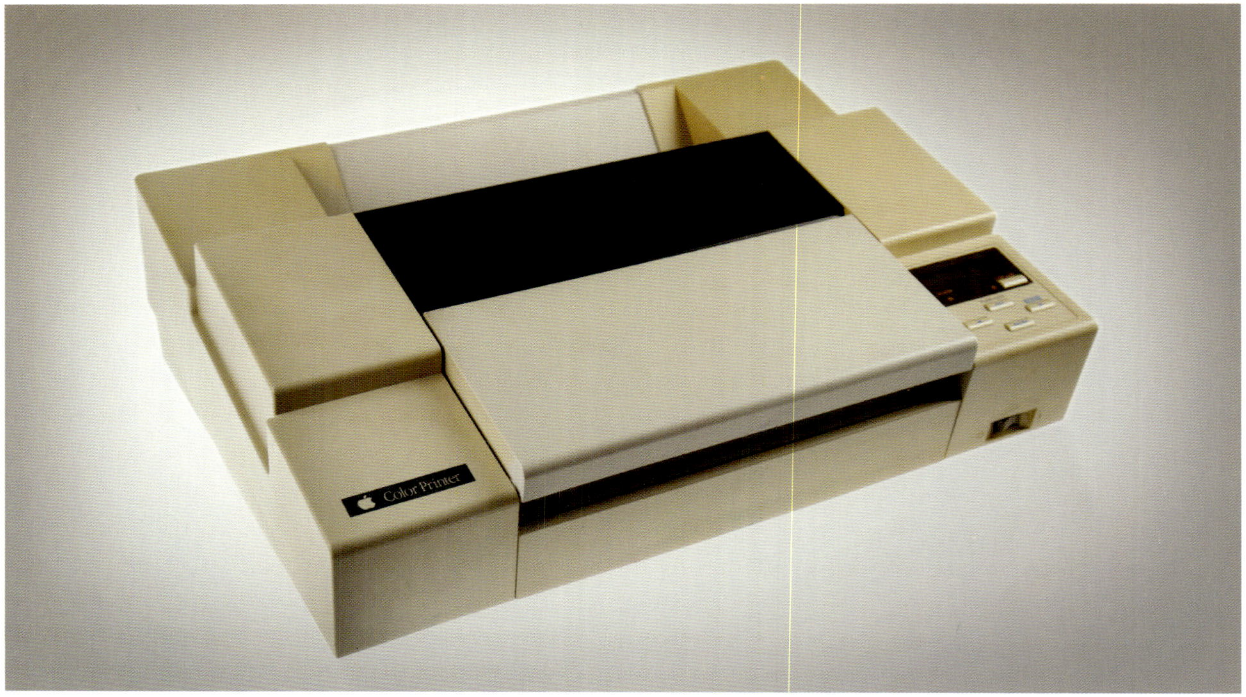

▲ Color Printer, 1993

Letter Quality Printer, 1983 ▼

Color Plotter, 1984 ▶

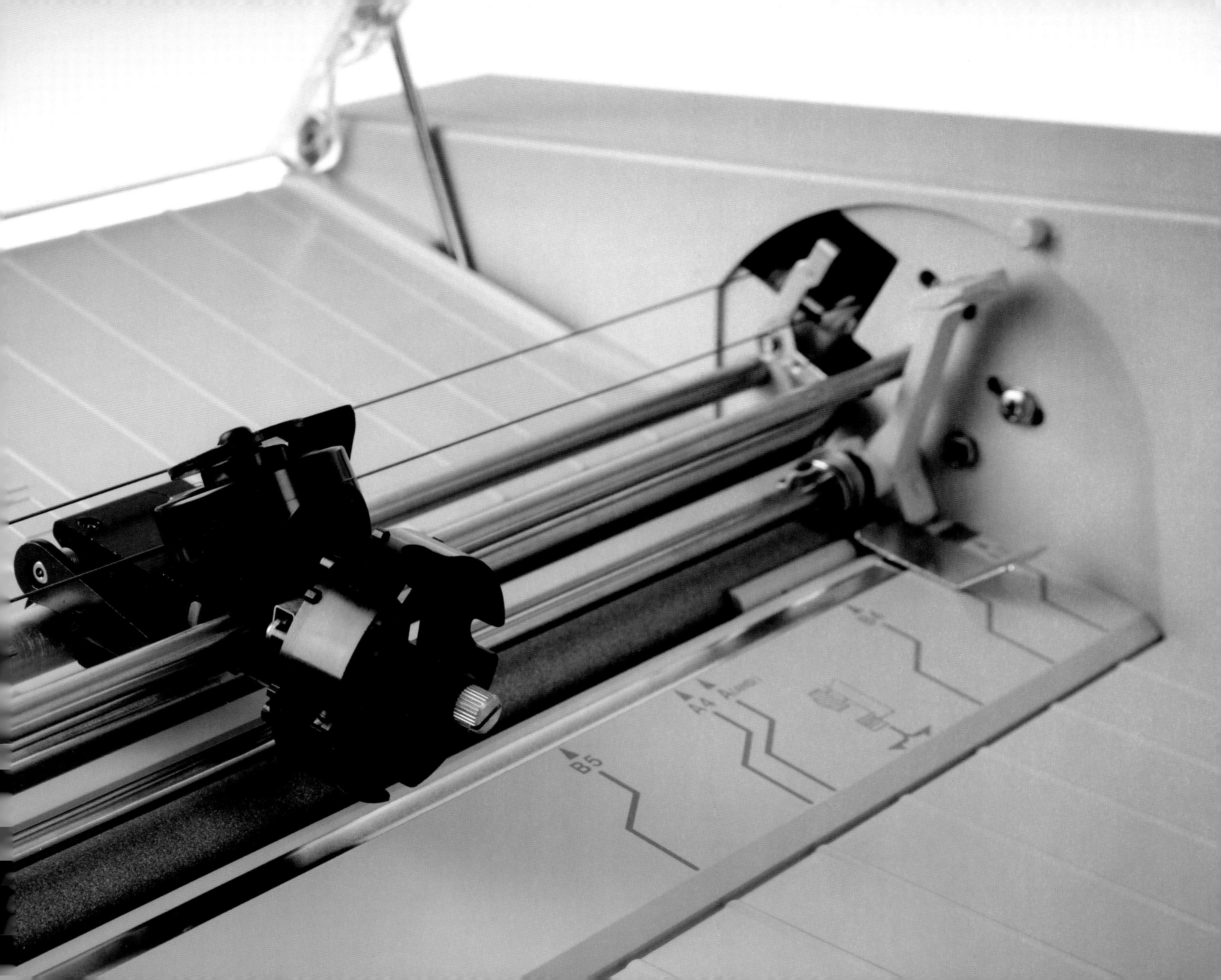
B5
A4

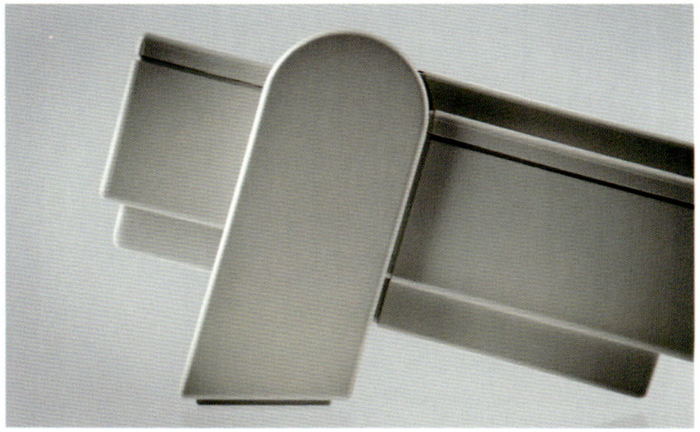

◂ ▾ ImageWriter II, 1985 ▸

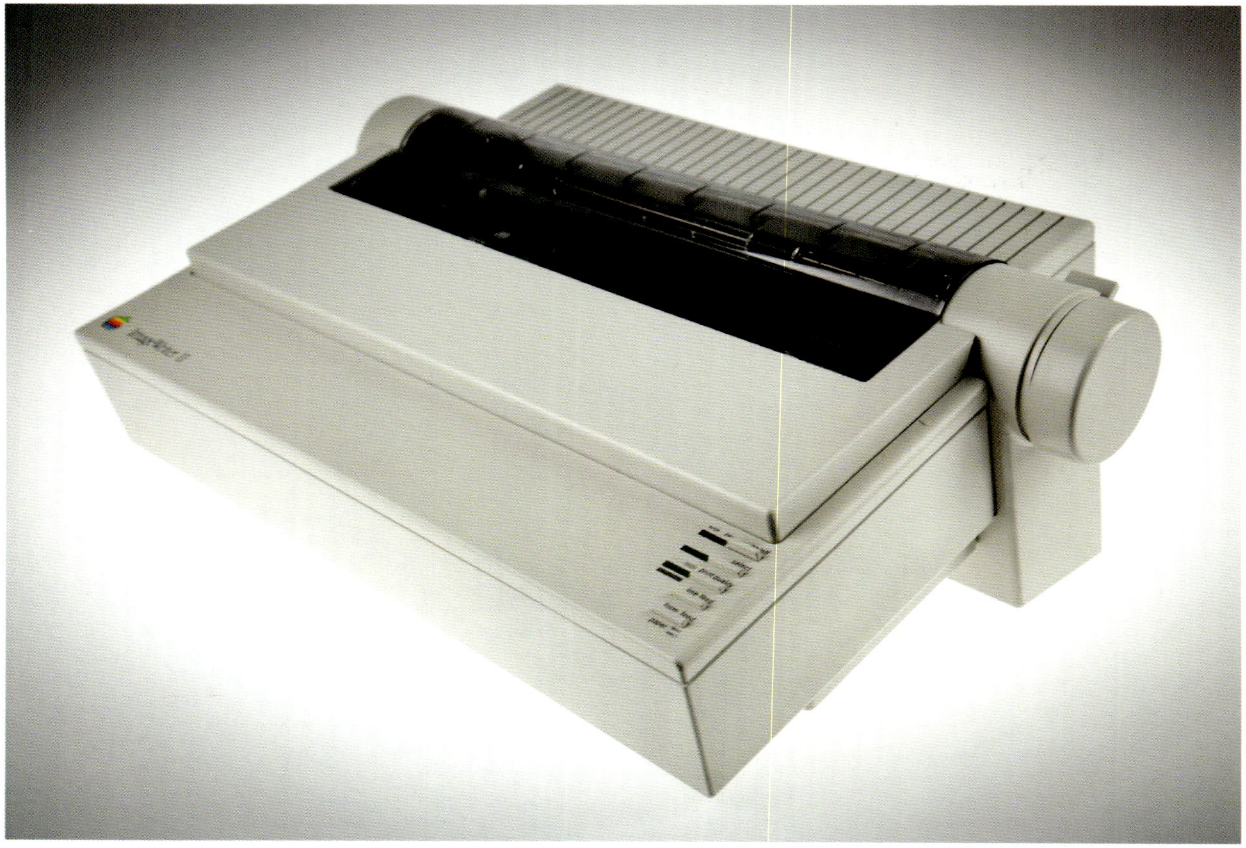

"I am always fascinated when I see the latest Apple products. Apple has managed to achieve what I never achieved: using the power of their products to persuade people to queue to buy them. For me, I had to queue to receive food at the end of World War II. That's quite a change."

—Dieter Rams

▲ Color StyleWriter 2200, 1995

▼ Color StyleWriter 4100, 1997; Portable StyleWriter, 1993 ▸

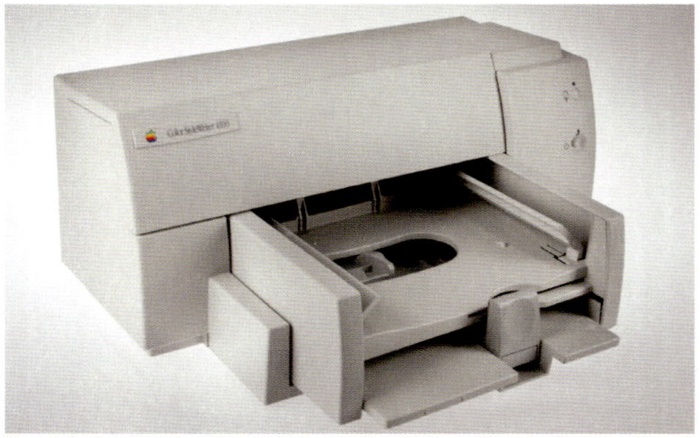

▲ StyleWriter II, 1993

▼ Personal LaserWriter 300, 1993

◄ StyleWriter, 1991

▼ LaserWriter, 1985

CONNECT THIS CABLE
ONLY TO THE APPLE
DISK][INTERFACE CARD
apple computer inc.™
10260 BANDLEY DRIVE
CUPERTINO, CALIFORNIA 95014
SERIAL NO. A2M0003-00001
MADE IN U.S.A.

◂ Disk II, 1978 ▸

▲ Disk III, 1978

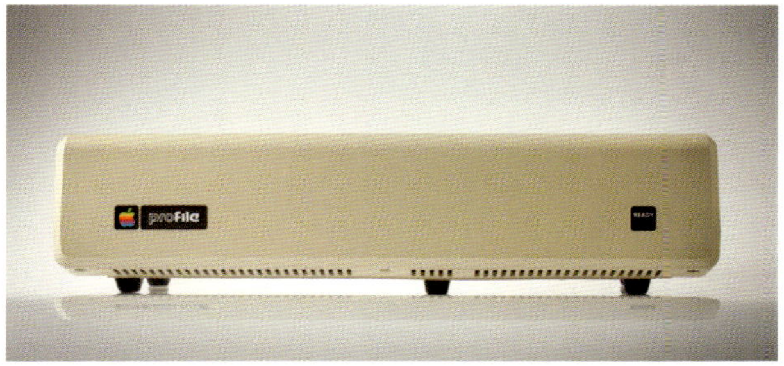

▲ Apple Profile, 1981

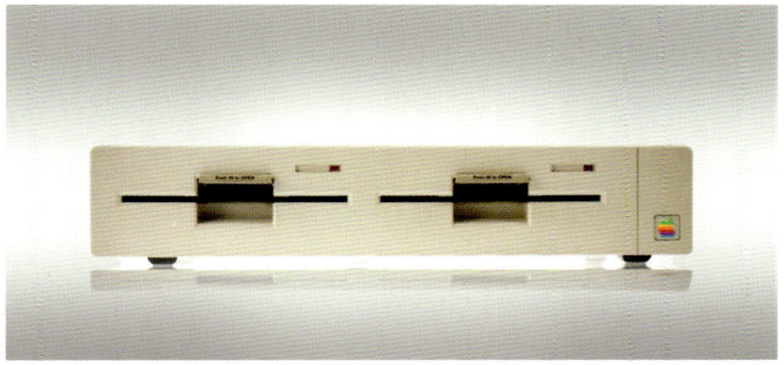

▲ DuoDisk, 1983

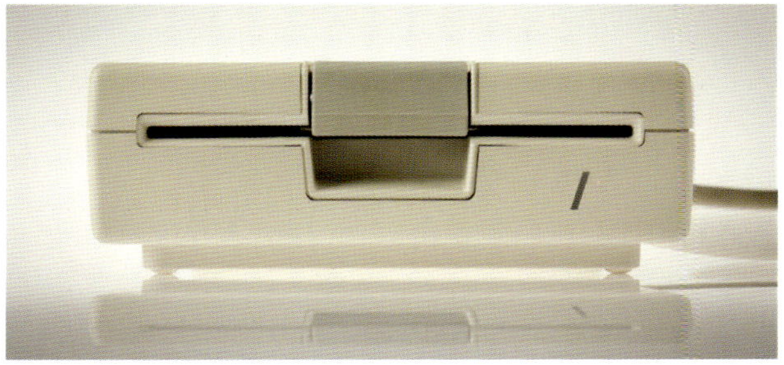

▲ Disk IIc, 1984

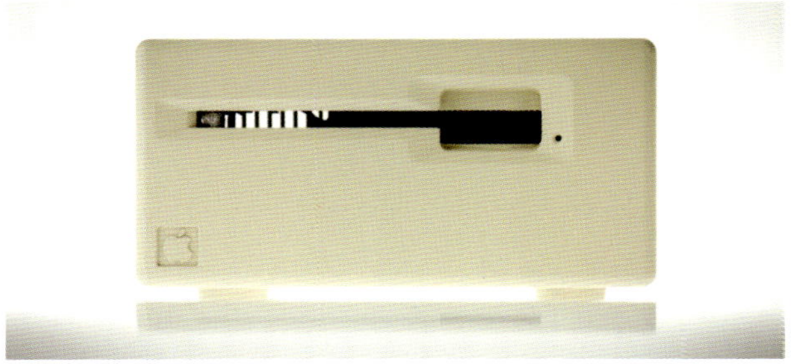

▲ Macintosh 400K External Drive, 1984

▲ 800K External Drive, 1985

▲ Macintosh Hard Disk 20, 1985

▲ Hard Disk 20SC, 1986

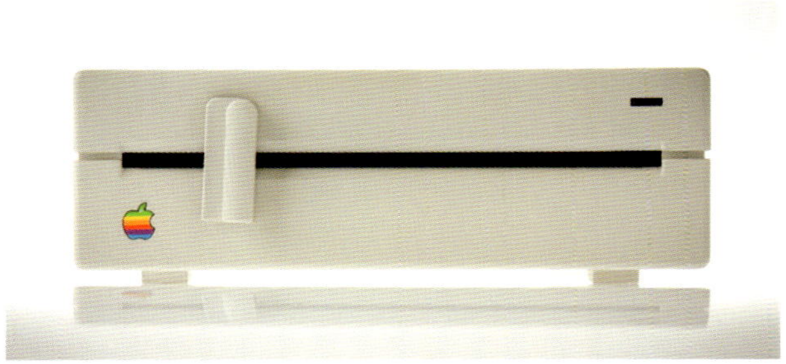

▲ PC 5.25″, 1987

◀ SuperDrive, 1991 ▲ Tape Backup 40SC, 1987

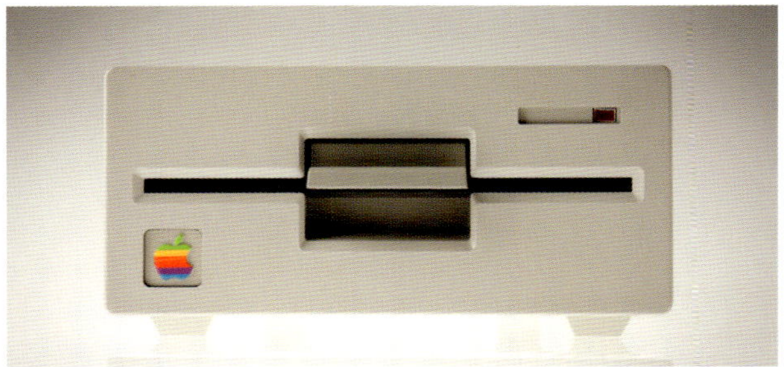

▲ 5.25″ Drive, 1986

▲ Apple CD 300, 1992

External Hard Drive 160SC, 1994

"Apple's products are unique not on their feature merits, but because of the way they are conceived, designed, built, sourced, manufactured, shipped, marketed, sold, opened, held, and used. This is integration taken to the extreme and it would be difficult for any company to replicate."

—Charlie Kindel, *cek.log*

Time Capsule, 2008 ▸

"I'd argue that Apple's push toward devices that are more about the human interface and less about the components is a form of a categorical imperative, a rule for acting that has no

conditions or qualifications—that there is no line, there is only an endless drive toward progress: more portable devices that get the job done with less thinking about the hardware."

—Nick Chaves, software engineer, nickchaves.com

▾ USB SuperDrive, 2010

"Sound is so important to the way that you experience an Apple product, so we wanted to make a headphone that was absolutely the very best it could be."

—Jonathan Ive

EarPods, 2012 ▸

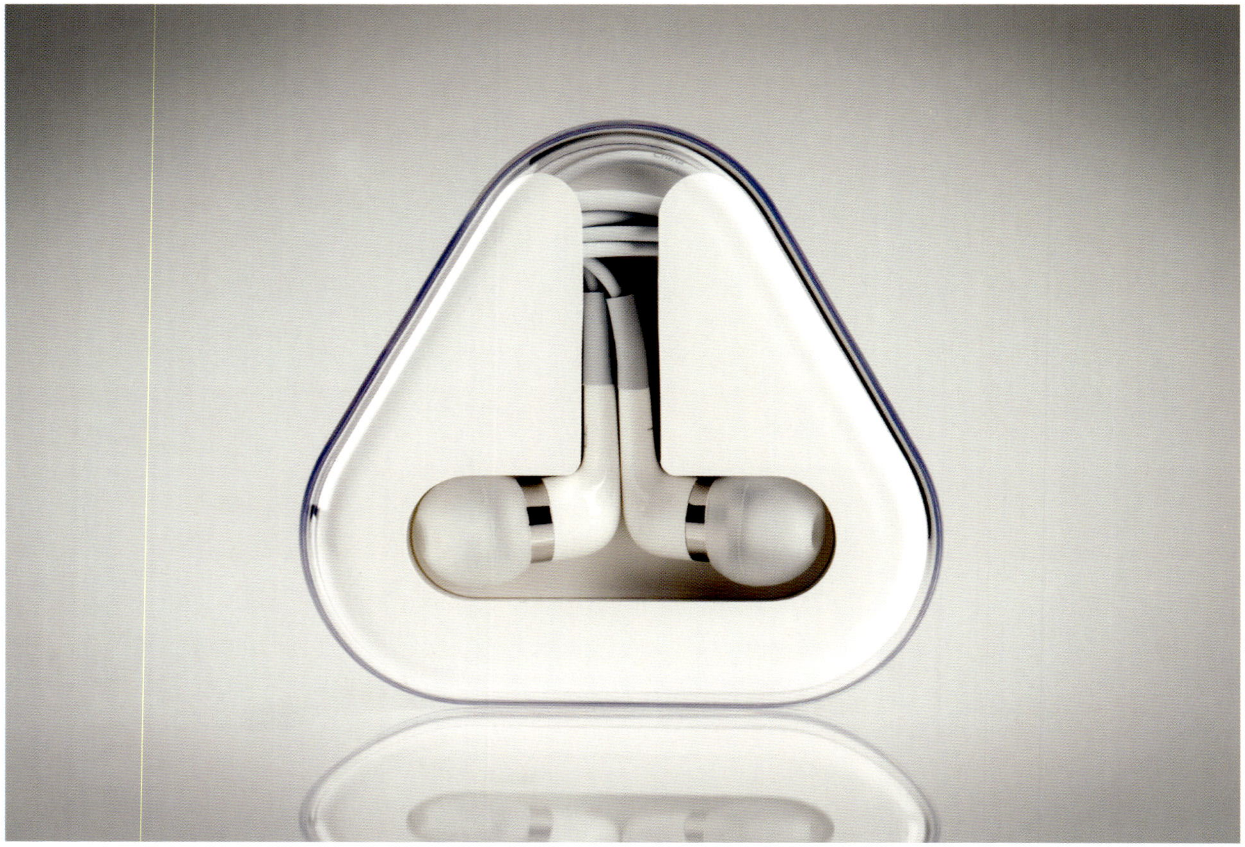

In-Ear Headphones, 2008 ▸

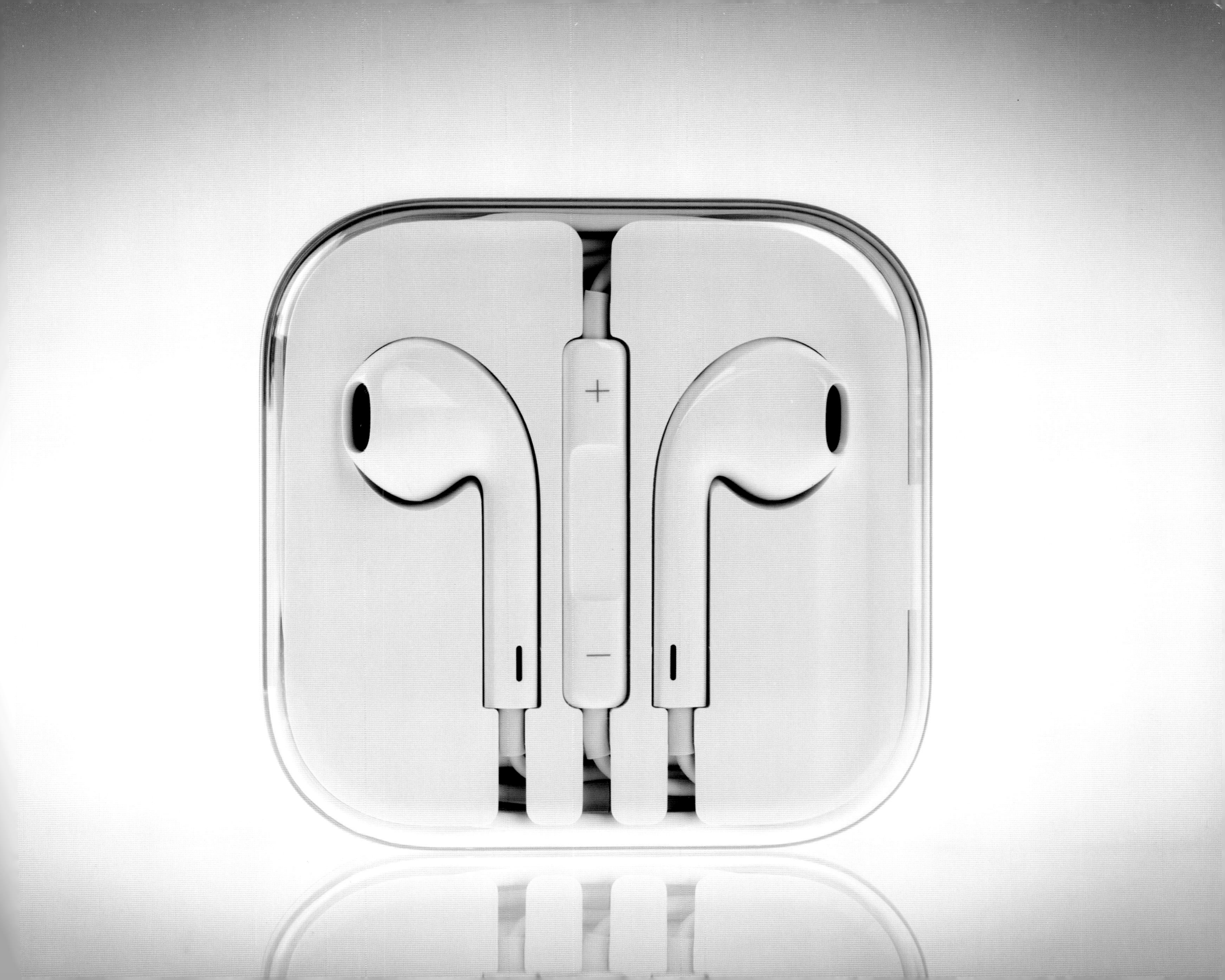

Chet Pipkin, *Founder, Chairman and CEO of Belkin International, Inc.*

I remember the day that the unit sales of unrecorded CDs outsold pre-recorded CDs (music CDs) at Best Buy. That's the day we knew that digital technology would completely disrupt how we listen to music, watch pre-recorded video, and, eventually, view television. What we didn't know was who would do it.

On that day, Apple wasn't the obvious choice that it is today. But Steve Jobs understood—better than anyone ever has—how people want to do things. It wasn't about taking a hard drive and wrapping it in a display, with controls and a battery. His appreciation for the total user experience, from discovering music, to buying it, storing it, and listening to it—completely on our terms—would change the world. His vision for photos, video content, communication, information, sharing, and connecting went far beyond music, but he got music right first. His understanding of the value of a complete ecosystem around iDevices completed the picture.

At Belkin, we don't try to develop the product that will be the tip of the spear for the market. We follow important products and look for what kinds of solution sets we will be able to contribute. Apple was a company that gave us that opportunity.

It has been amazing to be a small participant in Apple's totally transformational journey. It was fun to watch Steve launch the first iPod with the 30-pin connector, and the voice recorder that Belkin and Apple co-developed. Providing the extra battery pack that allowed the iPod to be used by US astronauts in space was a rewarding moment for me, too.

From the humble beginnings of a little device that delivered the listening end of a grand music vision, to the iPhone, which is almost anything but a phone, to the iPad tablet experience that is disrupting the entire PC marketplace, we have hardly begun to see the complete story of Apple's grand vision. Future chapters will be even more amazing than this one. Stay tuned.

iDEVICES

"If there was ever a product that catalyzed what's Apple's reason for being, it's this." —Steve Jobs

◂ ▸ iPod, 1st Generation, 2001

menu

Bono
Adam Clayton
The Edge
Larry Mullen Jr
iPod
Special Edition
U2

"The concept of the Apple iPod is successful not simply because all of its individual elements work optimally together as a product but because all elements of the overall systems were designed for music listeners."

—Hartmut Esslinger, Founder of *frog*, author of *Design Forward*

◂ iPod U2 Special Edition, 2004

◂ iPod U2 Special Edition, 2004 ▾

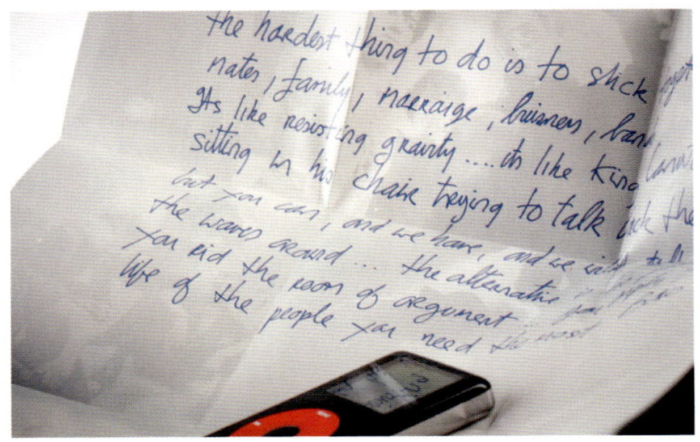

MENU

"Certainly, as a design team, I can't remember the last time where we were collectively lusting after a product as badly as we are after an iPod."

—Jonathan Ive

◂ ◂ iPod classic, 6th Generation, 2007

MENU

"Apple is a testament to the idea that 'little things matter.' Users may not consciously notice all the tiny bits of attention to detail they encounter in Apple products throughout a day, but it is what endears them to these products." —MG Siegler, investor/writer

◂ iPod mini, 2nd Generation, 2005

"I don't know who your product designers are, but boy, you're not paying them enough." —Moby

▼ iPod mini, 2nd Generation, 2005

iPod mini, 1st Generation, 2004 ►

iPod mini, 2nd Generation, 2005 ►

"Creativity is not a process, right? It's people who care enough to keep thinking about something until they find the simplest way to do it." —Tim Cook

iPod shuffle, 1st Generation, 2005

"From an insider's viewpoint, there really is no challenge Apple won't stand up to."

—Kelli Richards

iPod shuffle, 2nd Generation, 2008

"It feels almost inevitable. It feels almost undesigned." —Jonathan Ive

▾ iPod shuffle, 3rd Generation, 2009 ▸

◂ ◂ iPod shuffle, 4th Generation, 2010 ▾

"Oh my God. How could one company do all of this?"

—Tim Cook

iPod shuffle 3rd Generation, 2009 (six on left) ▸

iPod nano, 4th Generation, 2008 (nine in center) ▸

iPod nano, 5th Generation, 2009 (seven on right) ▸

MENU
MENU
MENU
MENU
MENU
MENU
MENU
MENU

"You ever wonder what this pocket's for? I've always wondered that. Well, now we know." —Steve Jobs, launch of iPod nano, 2005

iPod nano, 2nd Generation, 2006 ▸

▾ iPod nano, 1st Generation, 2005 ▸

iPod
Music
Photos
Extras
Settings
Shuffle Songs
MENU

iPod

"Apple's evolution in design is a great journey—from kids who thought 'let's build something cool' to something really sophisticated yet still cool . . . and I think that's been the magic of the company." —Ken Segall

◂ iPod nano, 4th Generation, 2008

◂ iPod nano, 3rd Generation, 2007

▾ iPod nano, 1st Generation, 2005

"iPod for Windows changed everything."

—Nobuyuki "Nobi" Hayashi, writer

◂ iPod nano, 5th Generation, 2009 ▸

"Apple today gives us good reason to rethink the link between brilliant design and dazzling profits." —Hartmut Esslinger

◂ iPod nano, 4th Generation, 2008

"Apple creates products that are hard to imagine, but once you have one, you can't imagine living without one." —Jonathan Ive

▾ iPod nano, 6th Generation, 2010 ▸

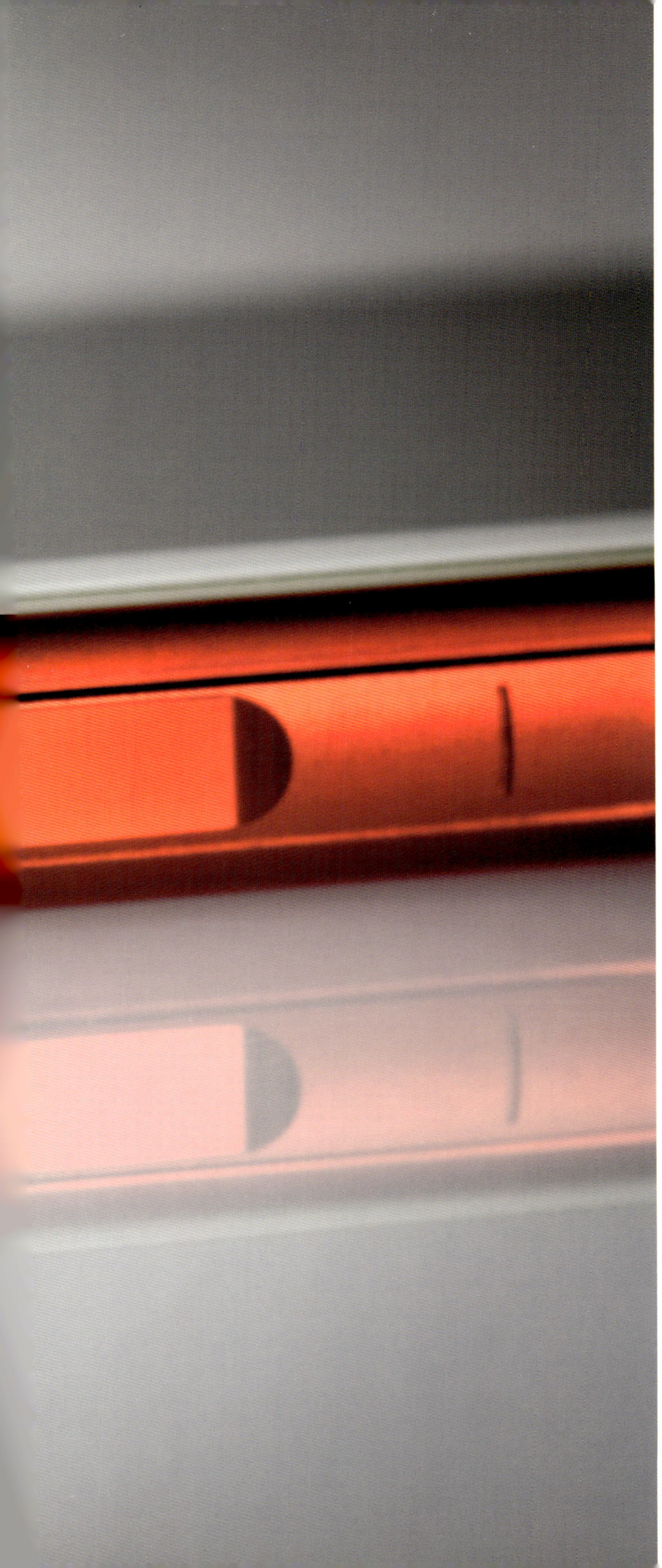

"OK, so what's not to like? Almost nothing, to be fair. ... It's amazingly portable, offers killer battery life, and connects to the richest media ecosystem on earth." —**Paul Thurrot, writer**

◂ iPod nano, 7th Generation, 2012 ▾

▾ iPod touch, 5th Generation, 2012 ▸

▲ iPhone Bluetooth Headset, 2007 ▼

▲ iPod HiFi, 2006 ▼

iPod mini, 2nd Generation inside an iPod HiFi ►

MENU

iPod mini + hp
6GB
Digital music player
Holds up to
1,500 songs*
For Windows® PCs
*Capacity based on 4 minutes per song and 128-Kbps AAC encoding.
iPod
iPod+hp
Includes an iTunes Music Store coupon for $50 off
The Complete U2
Digital Box Set
Requires broadband Internet connection
iPod
9:42 AM
Finally Made M

Music
Videos
Photos
Podcasts
Extras
Settings
Shuffle Songs
Now Playing
MENU
Videos
Photos
Podcasts
Extras
Settings
Shuffle Songs
Now Playing
MENU
iPod
9:42 AM
Corinne Bailey Rae
Put Your Records On
Corinne Bailey Rae
iPod
9:42 AM
John Lennon
Imagine
Lennon Legend

"Every once in a while, a revolutionary product comes along that changes everything."

—Steve Jobs, iPhone launch, 2007

iPhone 1st Generation, 2007 ▸

iPhone
Designed by Apple in California Assembled in China Model No.: A1203
FCC ID: BCGA1203 Serial No.: 5K828FHBWH8 IMEI No.: 011654000920281
8GB

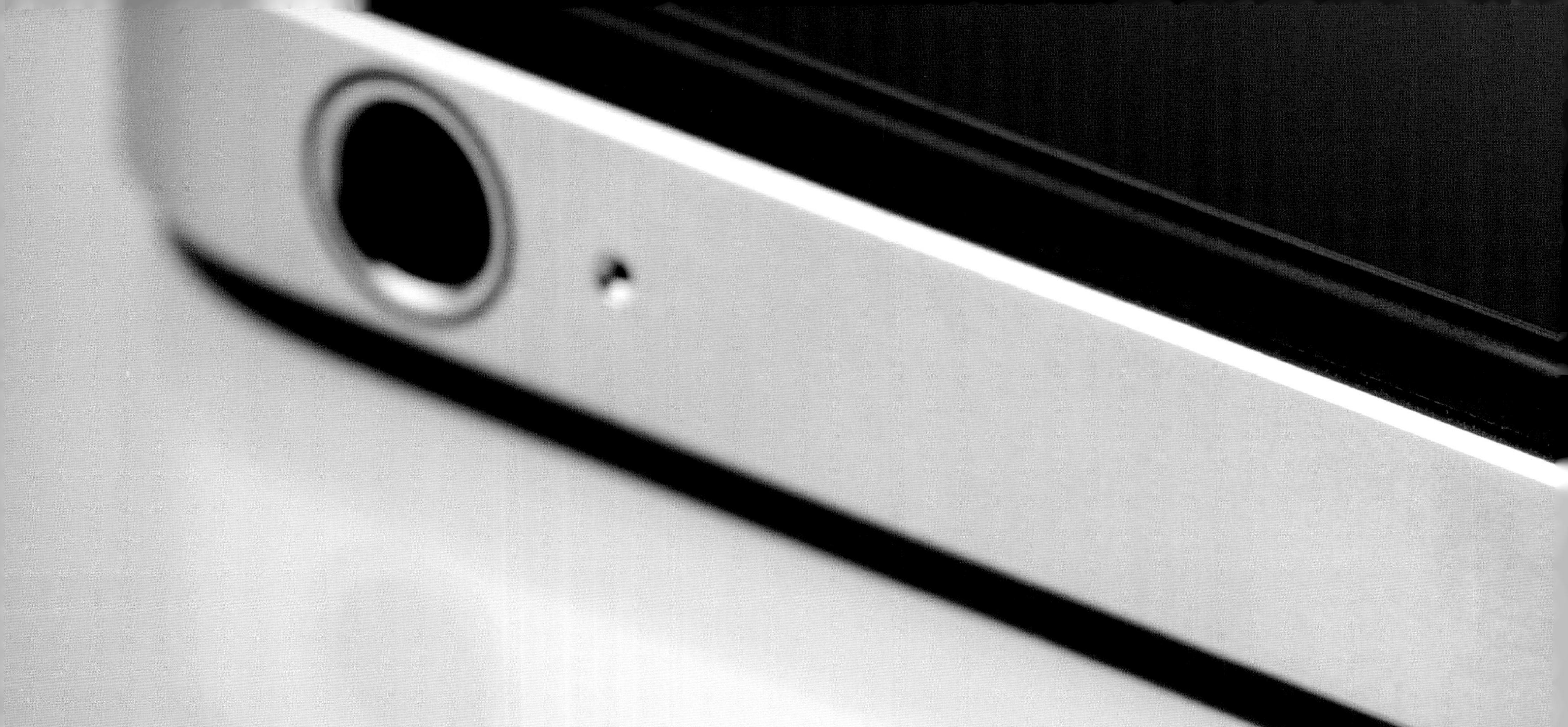

"The extreme simplicity of the Apple design is striking.
Overall it has undecorated flat surfaces with a plate of glass on the front all the way out to a very thin rim and a blank back. There is a crisp edge around the rim and a combination of curves, both at the corners and the sides. The design looks like an object the informed user would want to pick up and hold. It is an understated, smooth and simple product. It is a cool design."

—His Honour Judge Birss QC, Case No HC11C03050

iPhone 4S, 2011 ►

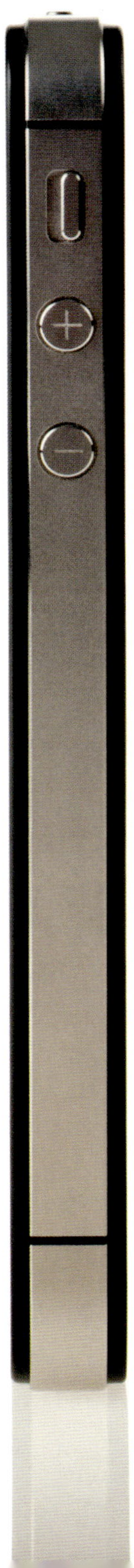

"I remember the first time I held an iPhone. I couldn't believe how small it was. How thin. It was so solid in the hand that it didn't feel built; it was closer to a stone you might find in a stream."

—Loren Brichter, Founder of atebits

◂ iPhone 4S, 2011; iPhone 5, 2012 ▸

"I don't think the level of invention has ever been matched by any other product we've done." —**Bob Mansfield, iPhone 5 launch**

◂ iPhone 5, 2012 ▾

iPad 1st Generation, 2010 ▸

"Some people have thought that [the third category of device] is a netbook. The problem is netbooks aren't better at anything. They're slow, they have low quality displays, and they run clunky old PC software. … and we don't think they're a third category device. But we think we've got something that is." **—Steve Jobs, introducing the iPad**

"You know, it's true. When something exceeds your ability to understand how it works, it sort of becomes magical, and that's exactly what the iPad is."

—Jonathan Ive

◄ ▲ iPad 1st Generation, 2010

iPad 2nd Generation, 2011 ▼

"We took the time to design a product that was a concentration of, not a reduction of, the original."

—Jonathan Ive

▼ iPad mini, 2012 ►

Tom Gilley, *CTO, technology strategist, entrepreneur*

Prototypes, proofs of concepts, and concept integrations are explorations into new ideas and the user experience, and ultimately influence product strategy. At Apple's core is its highly-guarded, top-secret prototyping team—a power-house of people that applies advanced techno-logical innovation to an iterative user-centric design process. What we see in big Apple product release events is the result of many proof-of-concept successes and failures. Prototypes that magically make their way out of Apple's labs command a mysterious allure and are truly lusted after by the technorati. They also give us a glimpse into what could have been, and perhaps the beginnings of what could be the next killer Apple product.

One of the most aggressive prototyping eras began with the success of the Apple portable products in partnership with the now famous Apple Industrial Design Group and the Advanced Technology Group (ATG). It was within ATG that my team imagined Apple products refined through competitive design iterations, user feedback prior to market requirements, and engineering specifications that would ultimately materialize into a product plan. ATG's experienced researchers and designers—all hungry for the latest research and technology to be applied to a mainstream Apple product—created a matrixed organization called the Concept Integration Lab. The Concept Integration Lab focused on accelerating the incorporation of advanced tech-nologies and methods into mainstream product plans. There were prototypes and concept inte-grations that did not ship as product, but many made it outside the labs to influence future products.

The act of prototyping was not bound to one group, and many Apple product groups are as competitive internally as they are in the market, and many prototypes were born from such in-ternal competitions. Regardless of the motivation, the end result of all prototypes and concept integrations was the pushing of boundaries and expanded awareness of what was possible.

PROTOTYPES

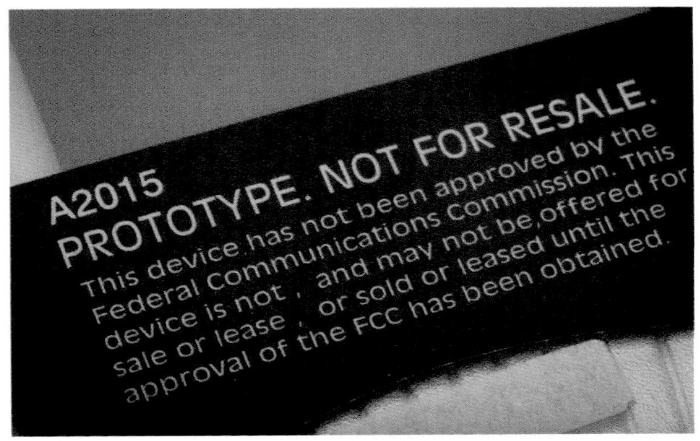
A2015
PROTOTYPE. NOT FOR RESALE.
This device has not been approved by the Federal Communications Commission. This device is not , and may not be offered for sale or lease , or sold or leased until the approval of the FCC has been obtained.

reset
esc
!
1
@
2
#
3
$
4
%
5
Q
W
E
S

"Embrace it. Change it. Improve it. Make your mark upon it."

—Steve Jobs, in the documentary *Steve Jobs: Visionary Entrepreneur*

◂ Apple IIc ▸

◂ Apple Macintosh ▸

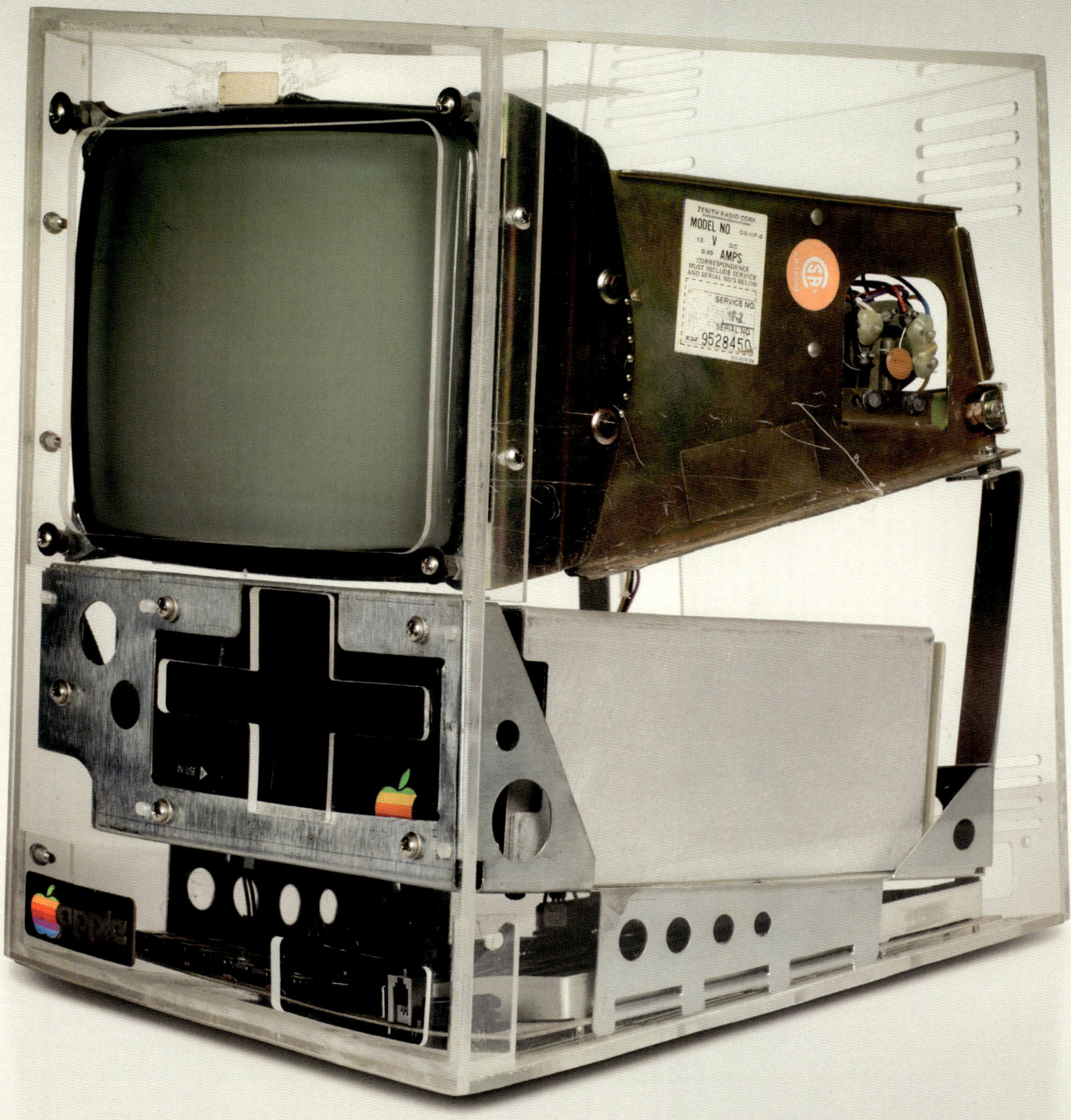
ZENITH RADIO CORP.
MODEL NO
12 V DC
0.90 AMPS
CORRESPONDENCE MUST INCLUDE SERVICE AND SERIAL NO'S BELOW
SERVICE NO.
SERIAL NO
9528450
IN USE
apple

"What I'd like to do this morning is recreate for you the impression I had when I took, for the first time, a prototype of the Macintosh Portable home, set it down, opened it, pressed a key and it woke up instantly and all my work was there."

—**Jean-Louis Gassée, launch of the Macintosh Portable, 1989**

◂ Macintosh Portable ▸

delete

Macintosh board

Macintosh

"I can still remember the first Mac that I purchased. I remember the excitement of getting it home, unpacking it and hearing that iconic startup chime the first time I turned it on. Even now, it gives me chills thinking about it. I've been a Mac user ever since."

—Neal A. Pann, architect

▼ Apple /// ►

◂ Macintosh 128K with Twiggy Drive

▾ Profile

◂ Newton MessagePad ▾

Apple /// ▸

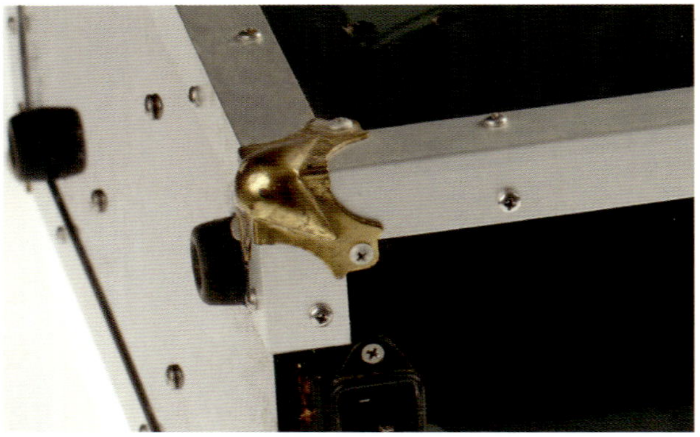

▾ Apple /// ▸

IN USE
disk II

"On a number of occasions we've actually all been honest with ourselves and said 'you know, this isn't good enough, we need to stop.' And that's very difficult."

—Jonathan Ive

Apple Pro Mouse ►

▲ Newton Bic

▼ Duo 3.5" Drive ►

California
Prototype
This device has not been authorized
as required by the rules of the Federal
Communications Commission. This
device is not, and may not be, offered
for sale or lease, or sold or leased,
until authorization is obtained.

◂ iPad 2

Newton Bic ▴

Apple Profile ▾

◂ Unifile Twiggy Drive

eMate ▸

undo
find
assist
light
scroll
delete
return
shift

"The eMate has a bright future—and it is for this reason that I am pulling it back into Apple—which has the resources to market and sell it much more broadly."

—Steve Jobs, September 9, 1997

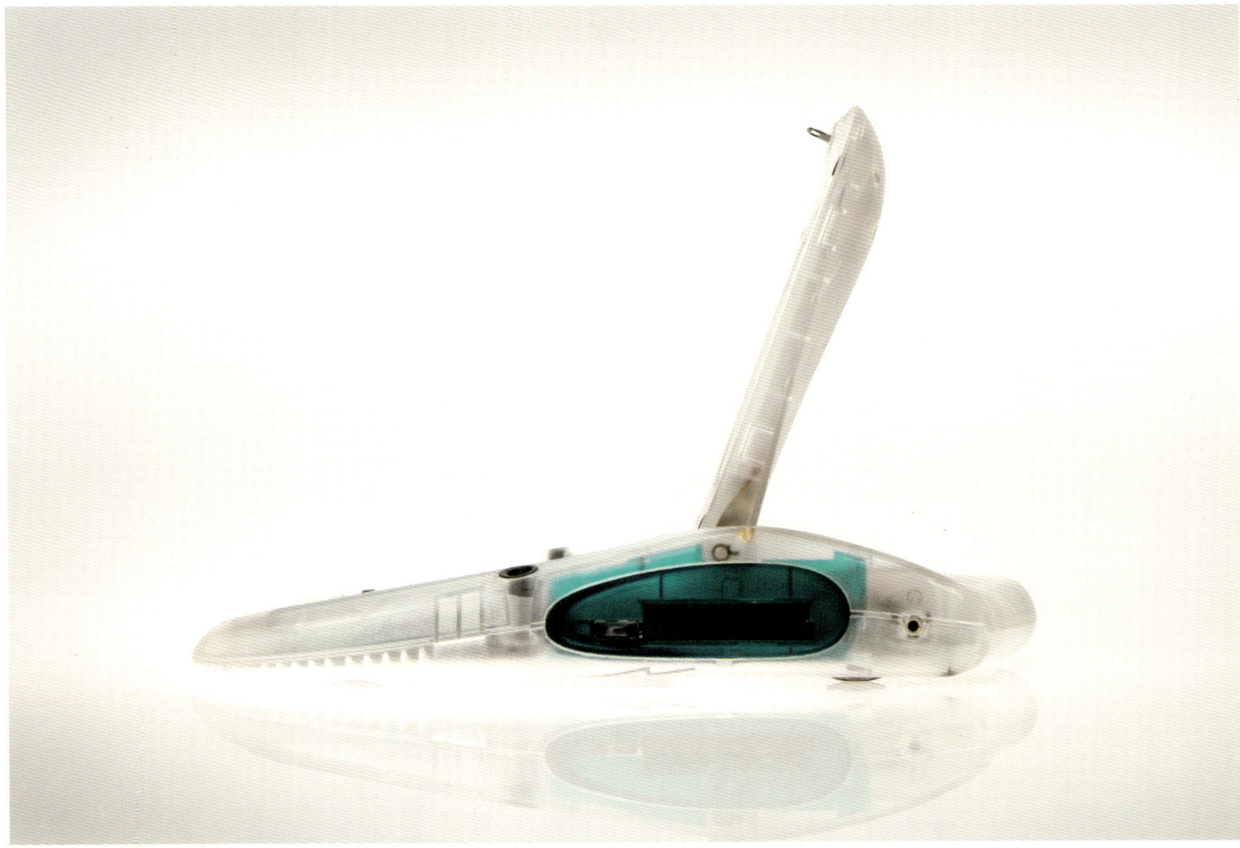

◂ eMate ▸

◂ eMate ▸

"If you think that Apple competes with Android, Windows, Blackberry or any other phone or tablet device, you're wrong. Apple builds on itself. Competition to Apple is what happens on the volleyball court during morning and afternoon break."

—Ken Hess, Windows and Linux system administrator

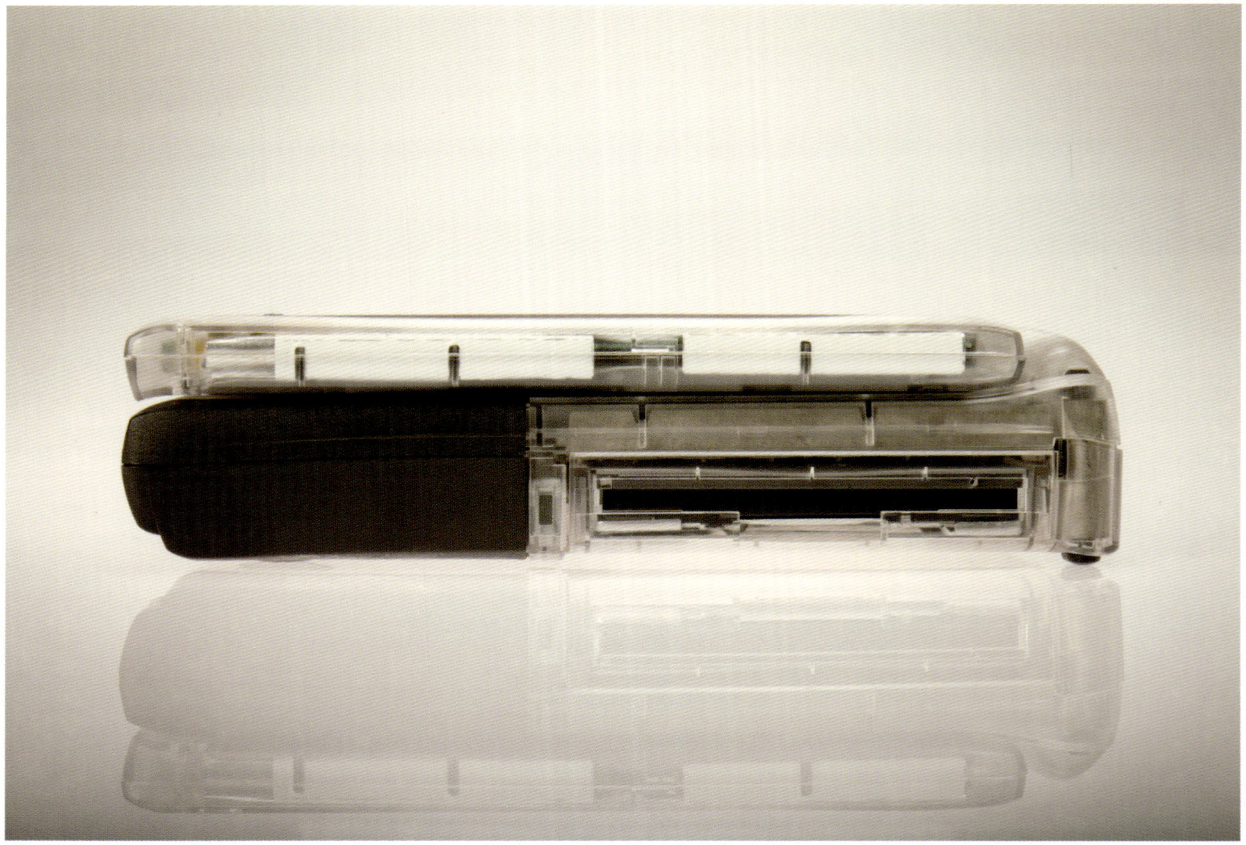

◂ Macintosh PowerBook 5300e ▸

N
M
L
enter
shift

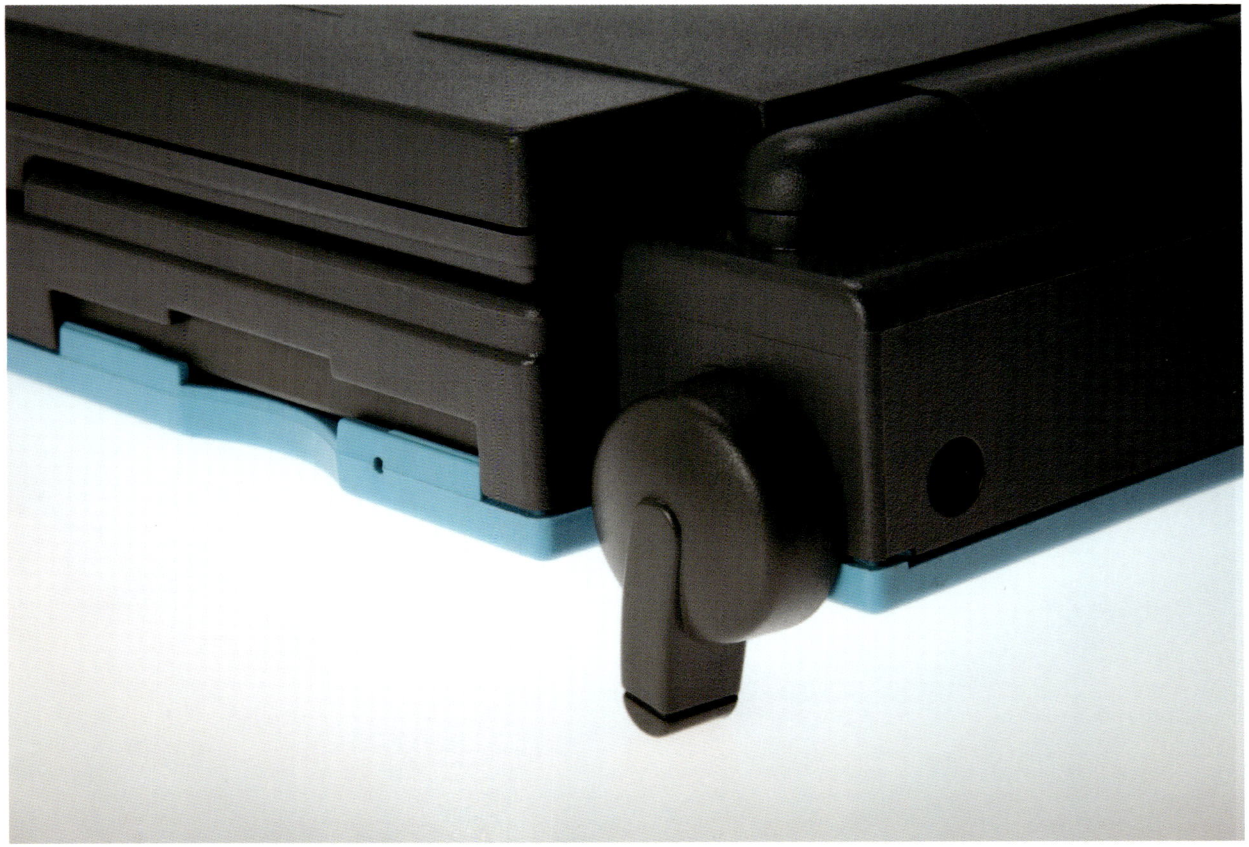

◂ Macintosh PowerBook 5300

Macintosh PowerBook 180c ▸

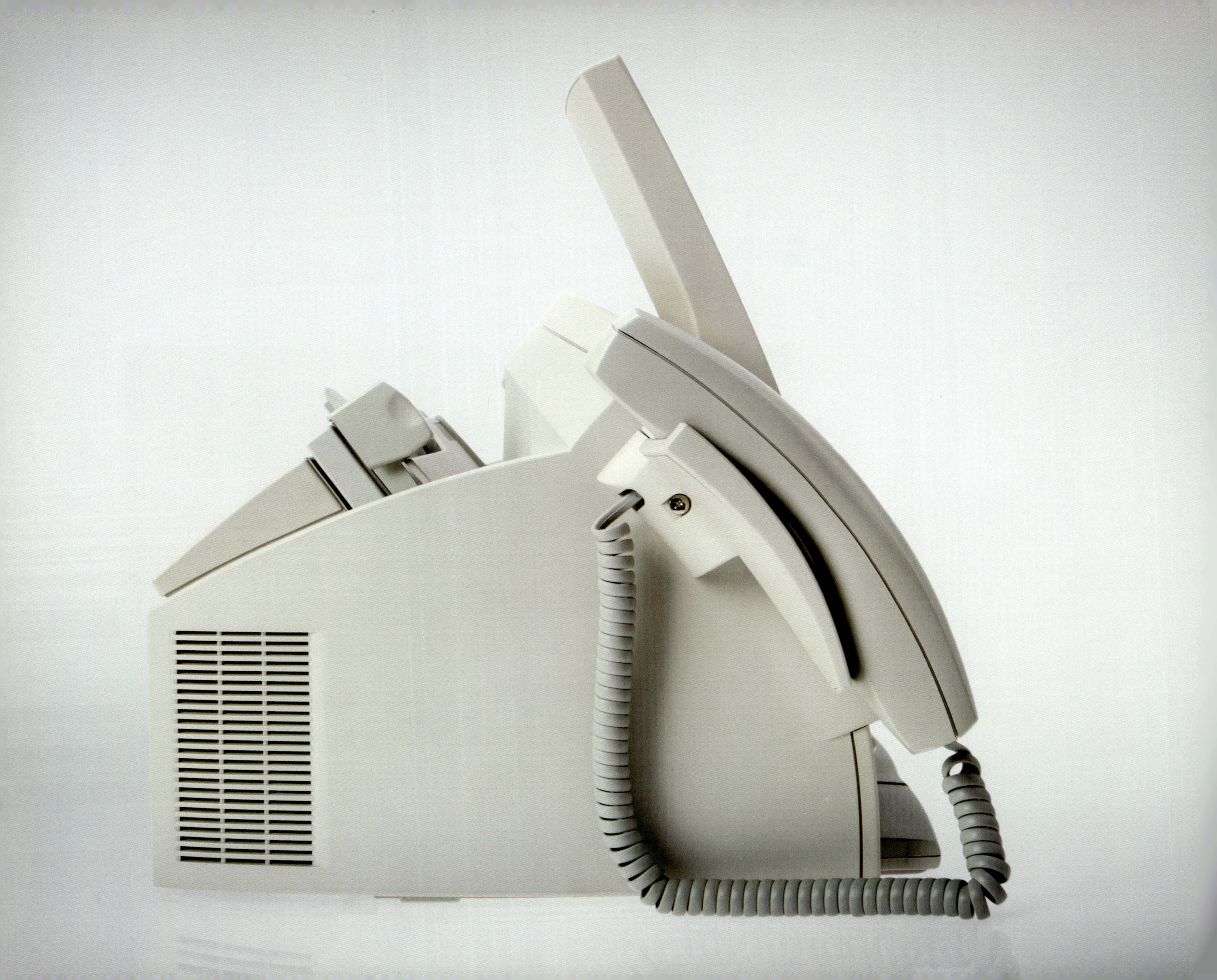

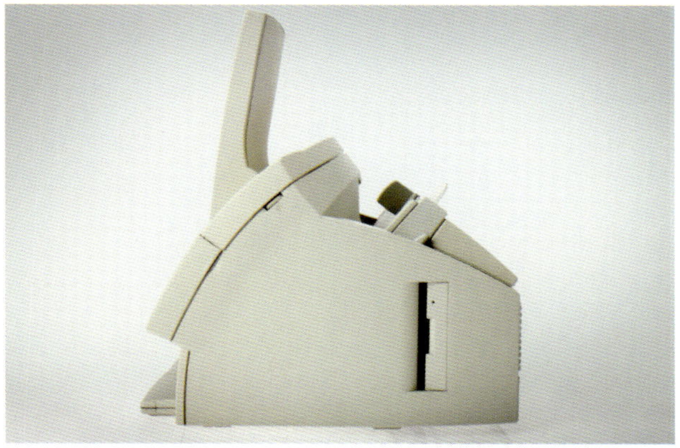

◀ ▲ Apple Paladin

▲ Apple Paladin ▼

▲ Apple Interactive Television

MultiServer ▼

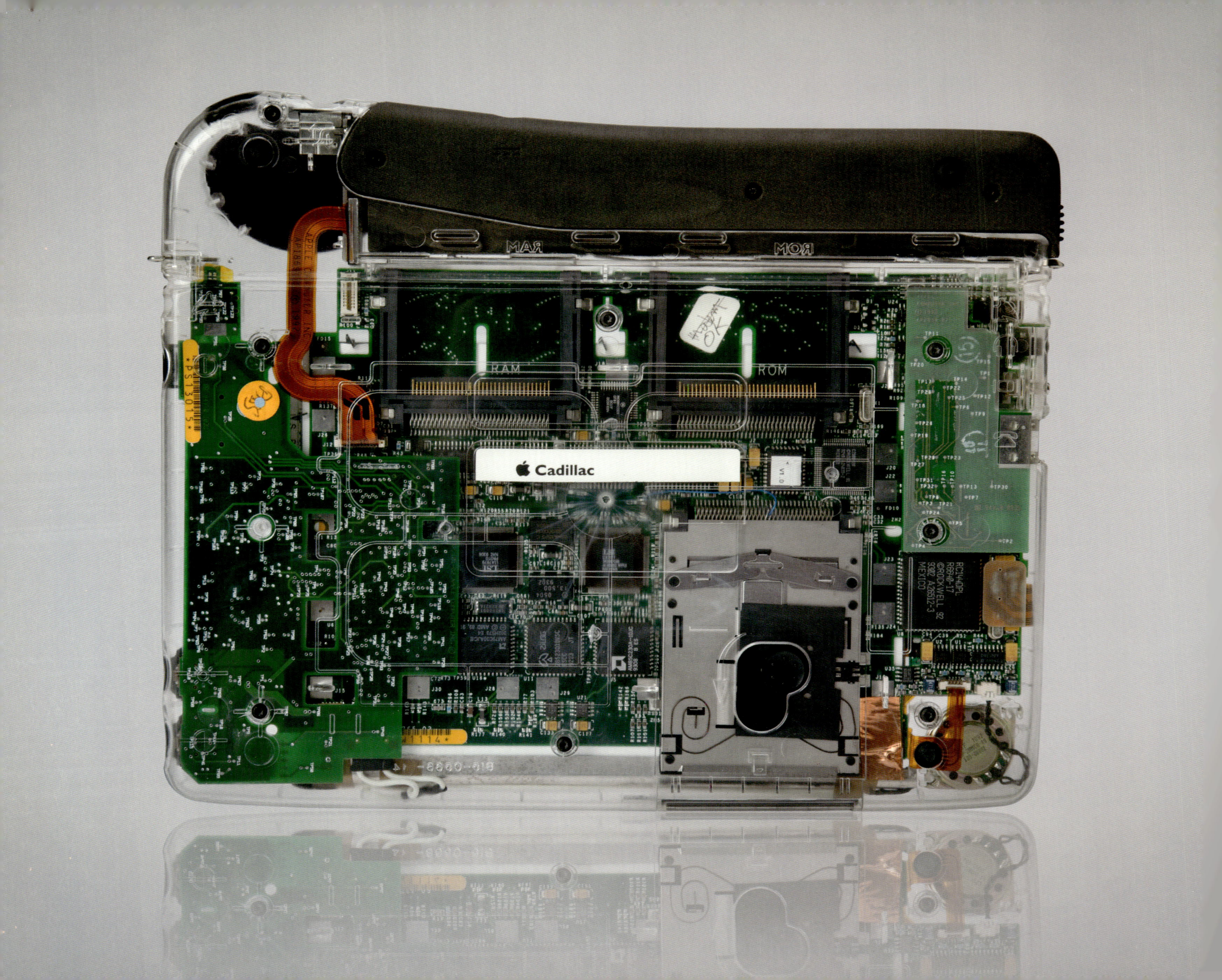
Cadillac
RAM
ROM

"It was a new way of looking at computers ... that recognition of the power of design that illuminated the path for Apple to move forward. From that point on, Apple found themselves in the revolution business—one amazing innovation after the next." —Ken Segall

◂ Newton "Cadillac" ▸

"The W.A.L.T. was an awesome device. We had such a small team working on it, but we were very devoted to it and wanted it to succeed."

—Randy Carr, former W.A.L.T. developer, Apple Inc.

◂ W.A.L.T.

Macintosh ▸

U32
U33
U34
U35
U36
U37
U38
U28
LS393
C24
U31
HM4864-2
PAL 16R8
U20
C11
C12
RAM
C13
C26
C22
C20
C17
C31
RP1
R24
U26
U27
EPROM/ROM
U10
LS126
LS161
PAL 16R8
U17
© 1982
C18
MADE IN USA
apple computer inc.
U11
C19
MC68000L10
GN78231
U58
U57
U4
U14
LS86
LS323
SY6522
Z8530
U9
U53
LS85
C21
LS169
U30
LS04
J8
U1
C28
U15
26LS30
FILTER
U47
R15
C29
R2
R1
C30
C34
26LS32
R11
R18
U59
Y2
R22
R23

"If something doesn't need to be there, it's not there. I don't know how we could make something any more essential, any simpler than the new MacBook."

—Jonathan Ive, launch of the MacBook Pro, 2008

MacBook Pro ►

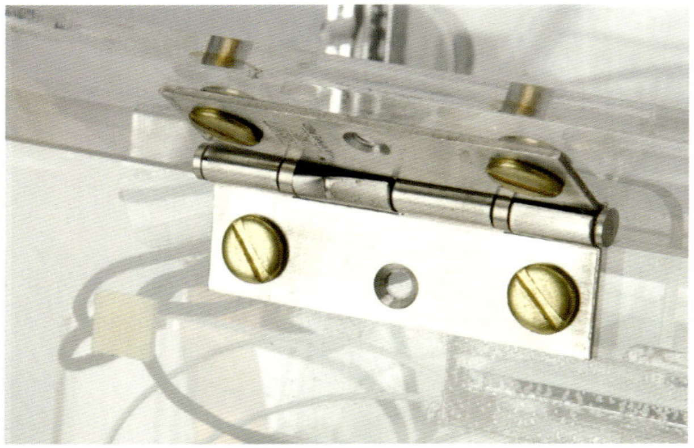

▲ ▼ MacBook Pro ►

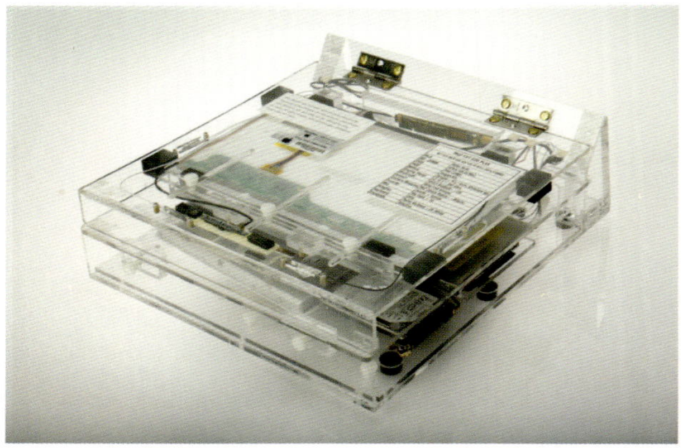

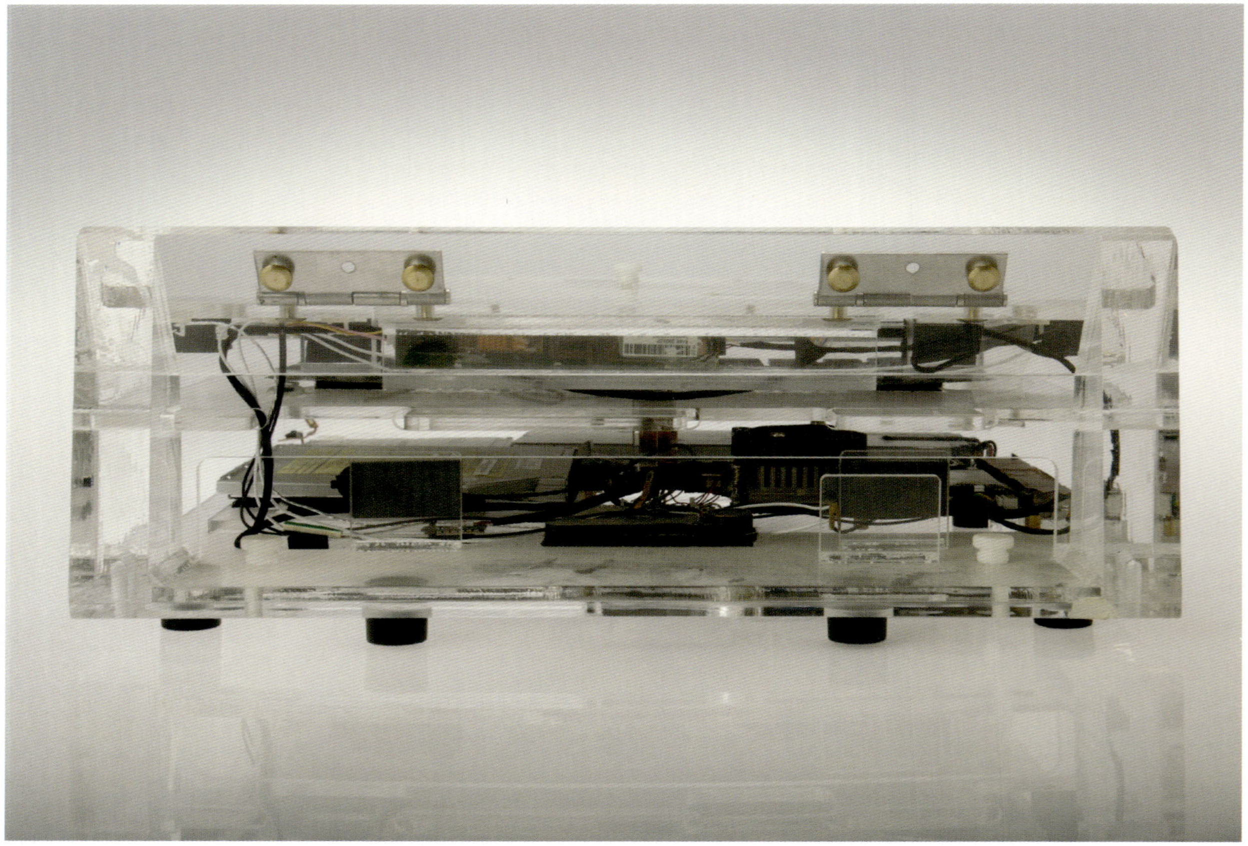

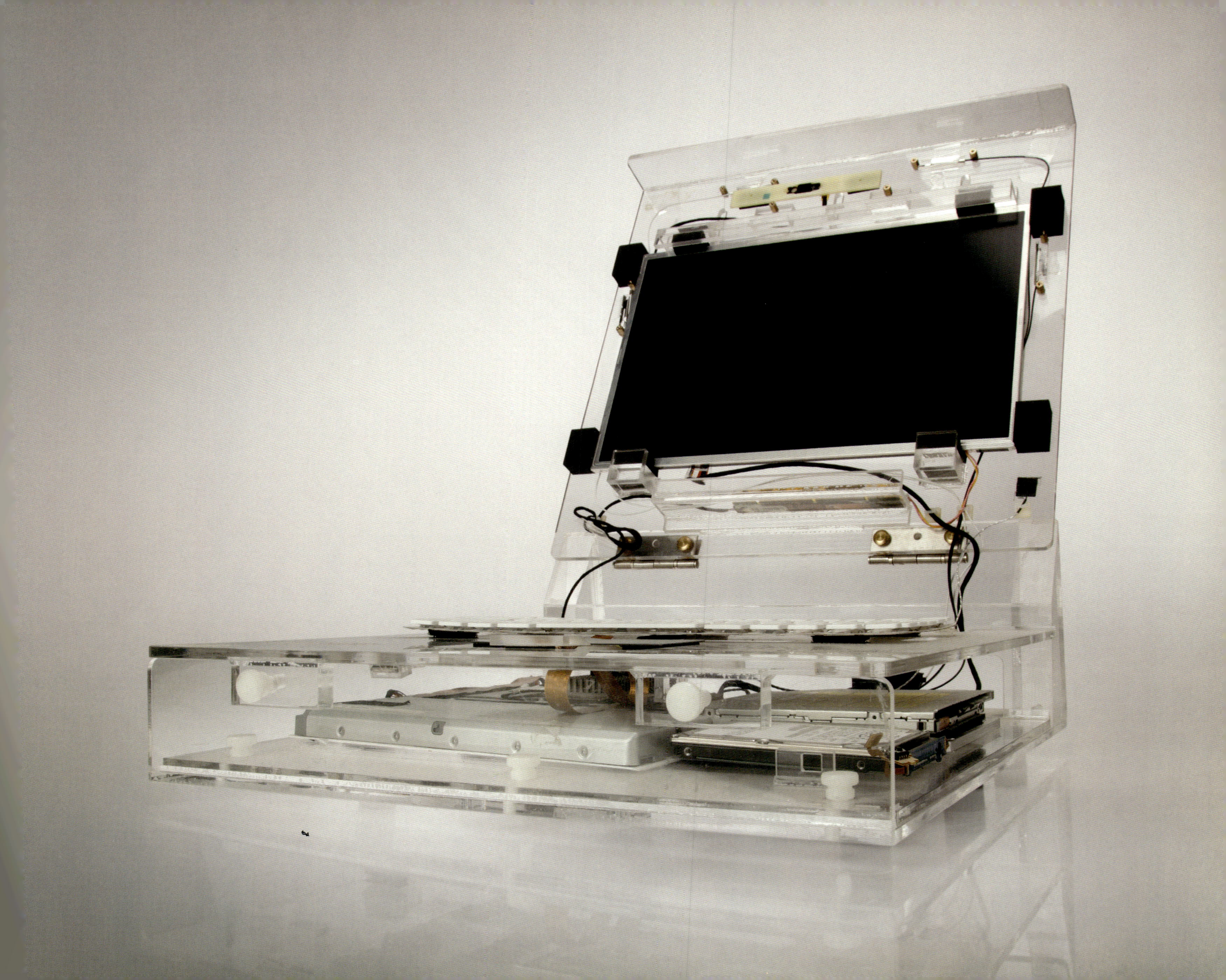

VLSI

"Ideas that were born decades ago are still coming to life at Apple."

—Kelli Richards

◂ "Pizza Box" Portable, built for Space Shuttle Mission STS-43 ▸

PenLite Prototype Unit-Not for Resale
Apple Computer, Inc.
Cupertino, California
Assembled in U.S.A.
This device has not
Federal
device is not, and may
sale or lease, or
proval of the FCC has

◂ Penlite Prototype ▾

Penlite Prototype ▾

▲ Penlite Prototype ▼

▼ Apple Scribe ►

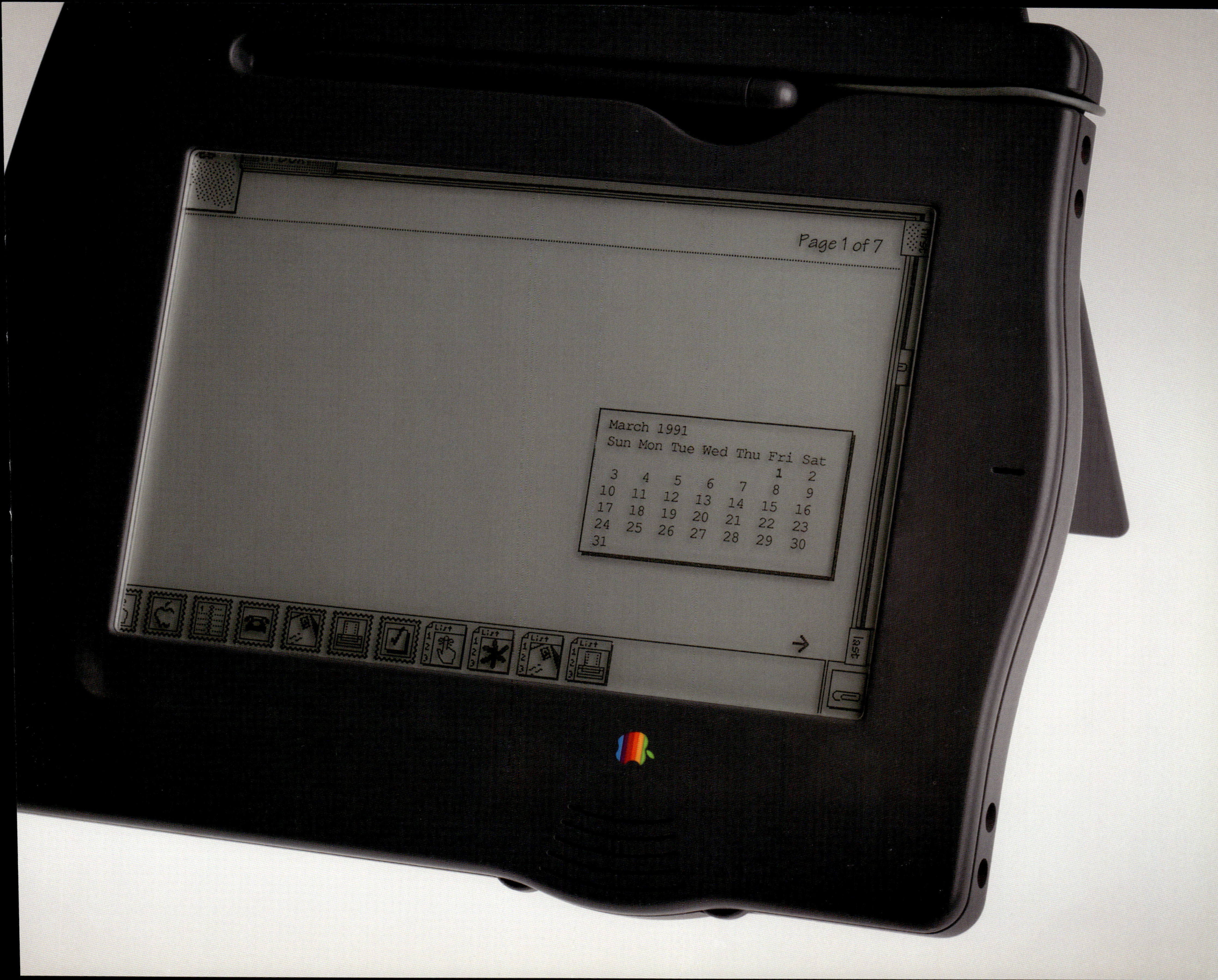
Page 1 of 7
March 1991
Sun Mon Tue Wed Thu Fri Sat
1 2
3 4 5 6 7 8 9
10 11 12 13 14 15 16
17 18 19 20 21 22 23
24 25 26 27 28 29 30
31
List
List
List
List
last

Sebastiaan de With, *visual designer*

Packaging is one of Apple's more curious and unexpected strengths. Some Apple detractors argue that Apple's packaging proves how much it favors style over actual substance. I say Apple is where it is because it has succeeded in delivering both, focusing on the total user experience. No matter who you ask, all will agree that Apple puts a remarkable amount of care into crafting simple, elegant packaging for its products, with the goal of giving the customer the end-to-end Apple experience.

As a young teen growing up in the Netherlands, I had been drawn to the lustre and design of Apple's Macs, but they weren't readily available back then. I remember the day I received my very first Apple product. It was a second-generation iPod and marked my first encounter with not only the excellent design of the product, but Apple's packaging as well.

When it arrived, I was surprised to find that the diminutive iPod came in such a large box! The box was made of perfect matte black cardboard, wrapped in a square cardboard sleeve with life-size product images and a tad of information printed discreetly on one side. As a less-than-easily-impressed teenager, I was rather blown away. Until then, whatever I'd bought had come in a typical box, with some instructions printed on cheap paper, and my purchase trapped in some plastic wrapping. I would quickly and unceremoniously unwrap my purchase, and throw the packaging away. But this was not your typical package. Apple had made the disposable . . . indisposable. There was no way I was throwing away that little box. It remained a permanent fixture on my desk for years to come.

Eventually, I was able to buy my first MacBook Pro, and its arrival met—and of course exceeded—my expectations. The packaging was sleek and elegant, designed for simplicity and ease of access. When they make it such an integral part of the experience, how can anyone throw it away? As I've learned over the years . . . even in today's disposable culture . . . not many do. Only Apple can make its packaging feel like a keepsake.

Apple's focus on the total experience of using a product—from its acquisition to its use to its retirement—continues to fascinate me. Each new product, including its packaging, is evidence of that continued commitment. Ultimately, each of us must say farewell to our favorites because it's time to experience the next Apple innovation. Yes, even though I've moved on, I still own and love my first iPod, and I thank that little black box for putting me on my professional design journey.

PACKAGING

"I think we have the responsibility to make great products that we can recycle and that are environmentally friendly. I think we have a responsibility to make products that have a greater good in them."

—Tim Cook

iBook

graphics tablet

Apple® Joystick IIe and IIc
For the Apple II, II Plus, IIe, and IIc
Apple® Joystick IIe and IIc

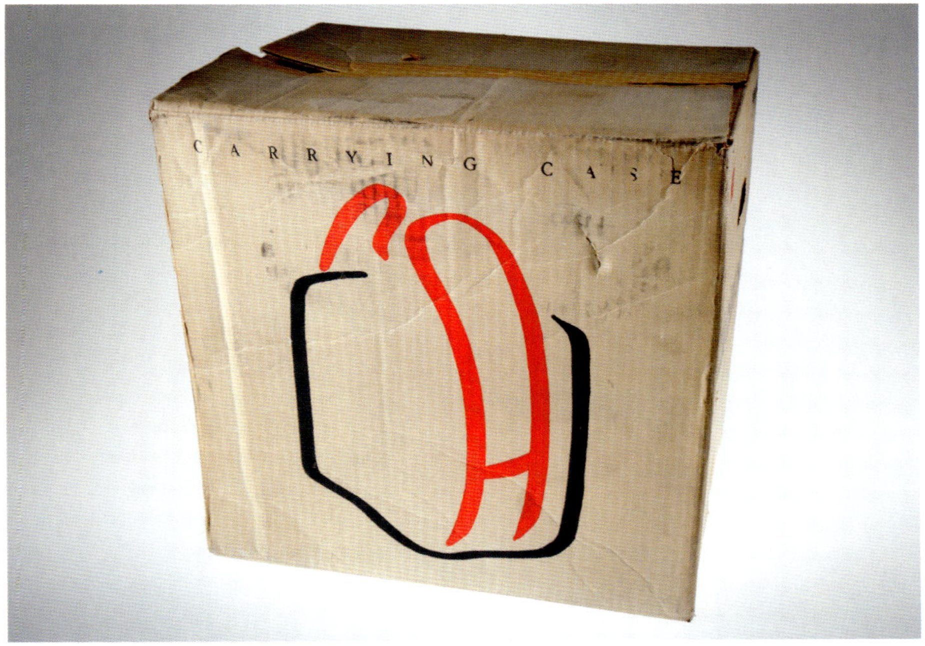
CARRYING CASE

Apple Adjustable Keyboard
Apple Adjustable Keyboard

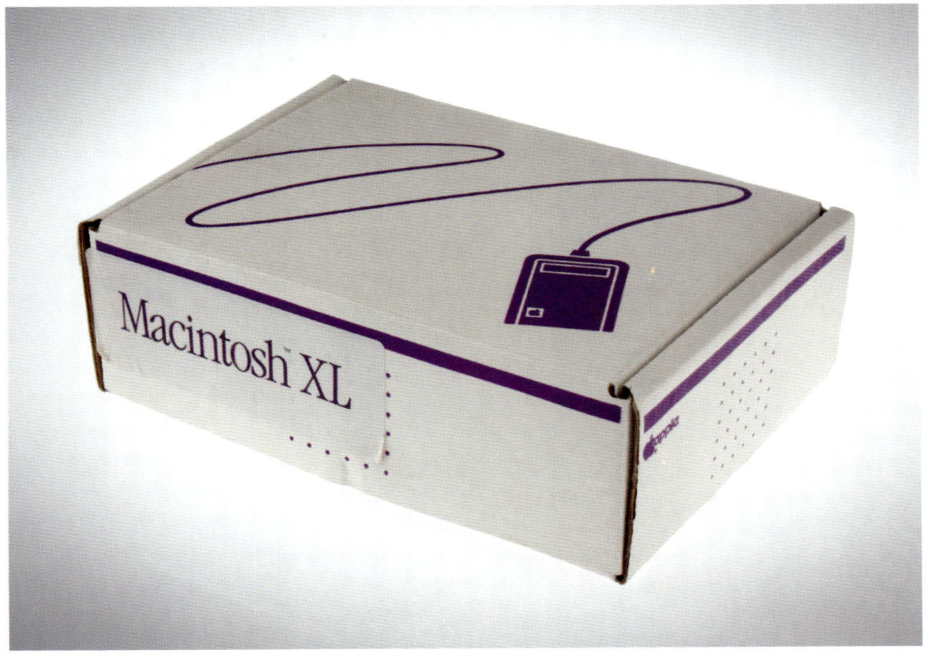
Macintosh™ XL

iPod

iPod
mini
4GB 1000 songs PC+Mac

iPod mini
Music
Extras
Settings
Shuffle Songs
Backlight
MENU
Actual size

Apple® IIe
Monitor and disk drive not included.

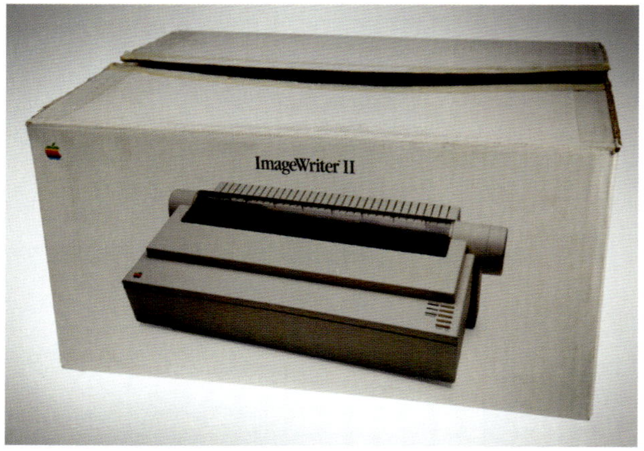
ImageWriter II

Alice
has slipped behind the looking glass onto a chessboard. The object of the game is to help Alice capture all of the chess pieces while avoiding her capture. The game is over when all of the opponents have been taken.
Alice can play with the abilities of any one of the six chess pieces. In the beginning of the game, six representatives step forward; a click on one determines Alice's skills. To make a move, click on a square. If it is a legal chess move, Alice will advance there. Clicking a few squares ahead is useful for hit-and-run attacks.
The score is decreased when Alice is captured and increased according to the strength of each piece taken. A perfect score of 999 is possible--Alice must never be captured and all pawns must become queens. Hit any key or the mouse button when ready to play. Hold the mouse button down over the score to get a menu.
Thanks to Marge, Andy, Bill, Bruce, Burrell, Larry, Patti, Steve, Jello and L. Carroll.
© 1984 APPLE
THROUGH THE LOOKING GLASS
STEVE CAPPS

Macintosh

iBook

iBook

iBook

iBook

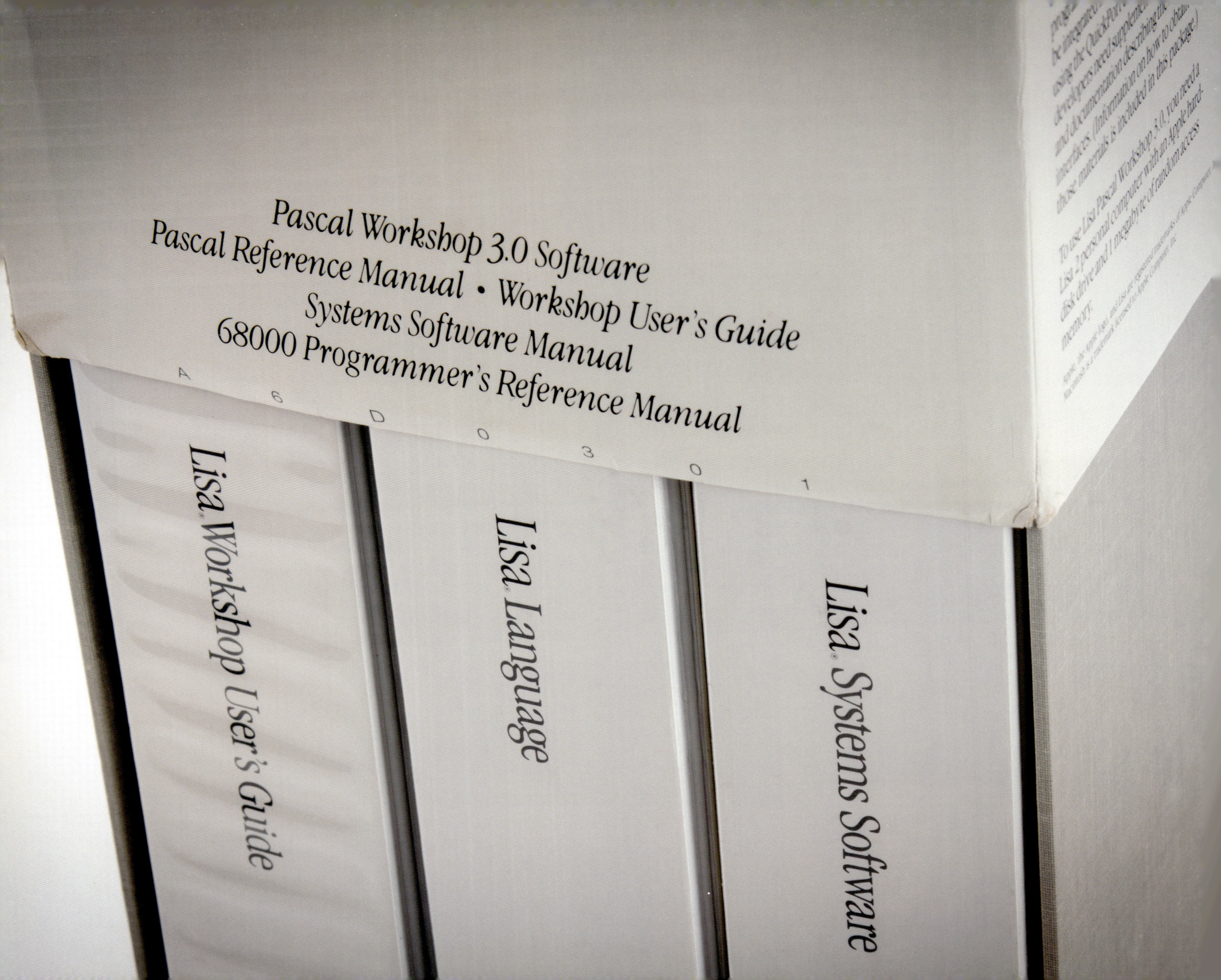
Pascal Workshop 3.0 Software
Pascal Reference Manual • Workshop User's Guide
Systems Software Manual
68000 Programmer's Reference Manual
A 6 D 0 3 0 1
To use Lisa Pascal Workshop 3.0, you need a
Lisa 2 personal computer with an Apple hard-
disk drive and 1 megabyte of random access
memory.
Lisa Workshop User's Guide
Lisa Language
Lisa Systems Software

Newton Keyboard
Newton
The fastest way to enter information into your Newton PDA.

Macintosh

Hand Controllers
IIe and *IIc*
Apple

Apple SuperDrive

Macintosh

Mac OS 8
Mac OS 8.5
AirPort Extreme
Apple Macintosh Portable
Mac OS 9
Here's your new 28,800-bps modem, speakerphone, fax, answering machine, and Internet launchpad.
AirPort Base Station
iPhone
A/UX
Programming Manuals
Macintosh Essentials
QuickTake AC Adapter
iPad
Apple IIc
Apple IIc Plus
Apple MPEG Media System
Apple Notebook Disks
MacBook Air
Macintosh Plus
QuickDraw 3D Accelerator Card
Work in 3D on your Macintosh faster than ever before.
Newton
AppleDesign Powered Speakers II
AirPort Express
802.11n Wi-Fi
Color LaserWriter Photoconductor Replacement Kit

Macintosh Color Display
Time Capsule
Apple IIe
Apple TV/Video System
Bonus!
Watch TV, capture video images, and create multimedia—all on your Macintosh.
Macintosh PowerBook G3
Apple 5.25 Drive
COLOR PLOTTER
PowerBook
MessagePad 120
iPod 15GB
Mac mini
iPod Special Edition U2
Mac Pro
Joystick IIe
A/UX Manuals
A portable, three-in-one CD player for your personal computer, television, and audio system
CDs Included
PowerCD
A/UX Manuals
Apple 5.25 Controller
numeric keypad IIe
FRAGILE
MacBook Pro
A/UX

US00D621256S

(12) **United States Design Patent**
Andre et al.

(10) **Patent No.: US D621,256 S**
(45) **Date of Patent: ** Aug. 10, 2010**

(54) **PACKAGING**

(75) Inventors: **Bartley K. Andre**, Menlo Park, CA (US); **Daniel J. Coster**, San Francisco, CA (US); **Daniele De Iuliis**, San Francisco, CA (US); **Richard P. Howarth**, San Francisco, CA (US); **Jonathan P. Ive**, San Francisco, CA (US); **Steve Jobs**, Palo Alto, CA (US); **Duncan Robert Kerr**, San Francisco, CA (US); **Shin Nishibori**, San Francisco, CA (US); **Matthew Dean Rohrbach**, San Francisco, CA (US); **Peter Russell-Clarke**, San Francisco, CA (US); **Douglas B. Satzger**, Menlo Park, CA (US); **Christopher J. Stringer**, Portola Valley, CA (US); **Eugene Antony Whang**, San Francisco, CA (US); **Rico Zorkendorfer**, San Francisco, CA (US)

(73) Assignee: **Apple Inc.**, Cupertino, CA (US)

(**) Term: **14 Years**

(21) Appl. No.: **29/284,343**

(22) Filed: **Sep. 5, 2007**

(51) **LOC (9) Cl.** **09-03**
(52) **U.S. Cl.** **D9/432**
(58) **Field of Classification Search** D9/430–433, D9/414, 418, 420–423, 529, 560; 206/278, 206/297, 299, 433, 457, 770, 737, 769, 776, 206/777, 778, 320; 229/100, 101, 103.3, 229/106, 107, 108, 108.1, 109, 110, 112, 229/116, 116.5, 117, 117.01, 117.03–117.08, 229/121, 122, 122.24, 122.29, 125.015, 126, 229/152, 181.1, 185.1, 186, 201, 917, 922, 229/923, 930–933, 935, 937, 939, 942; 220/796
See application file for complete search history.

(56) **References Cited**

U.S. PATENT DOCUMENTS

1,315,593	A		9/1919	Binder	
D106,245	S	*	9/1937	Young	D9/418
D111,649	S		10/1938	Di Domenico	
D114,891	S		5/1939	Fogel	
2,316,384	A	*	4/1943	Abramson	229/122.31
D159,157	S	*	6/1950	Koester	D9/757
D162,551	S	*	3/1951	Levine	D9/424
2,565,939	A	*	8/1951	Wriston	220/4.23
2,606,708	A	*	8/1952	Irvan	220/796
D167,689	S	*	9/1952	Hommer	D9/415
D191,070	S	*	8/1961	McCreary	D9/431
D246,439	S		11/1975	Lynn et al.	
D248,621	S		7/1978	Hay et al.	
D261,234	S	*	10/1981	Abraham	D9/432
D292,839	S	*	11/1987	Brogdon	D99/1
D309,431	S	*	7/1990	Sheehan	D9/424
5,358,101	A	*	10/1994	Lombardi	206/776
D368,429	S	*	4/1996	Serio, Jr.	D9/431
D368,588	S	*	4/1996	Goraleski et al.	D6/300
D369,295	S	*	4/1996	Kobari et al.	D9/423
D389,639	S	*	1/1998	Priebe	D3/203.8
D394,386	S	*	5/1998	Fischer	D9/432
D396,154	S	*	7/1998	Matthews	D6/470
D397,552	S		9/1998	Rutledge	
D406,463	S		3/1999	Rutledge	
D411,448	S		6/1999	Baker	
D417,391	S		12/1999	Szczepanski et al.	
D428,860	S	*	8/2000	Siperek	D13/182
6,234,308	B1	*	5/2001	Saffron et al.	206/316.2
6,289,655	B1	*	9/2001	Ridgeway et al.	53/449
6,400,247	B1	*	6/2002	King	335/302
D496,585	S	*	9/2004	McBride et al.	D9/423
D503,042	S	*	3/2005	Gutierrez et al.	D3/302
6,889,839	B1	*	5/2005	Rosten et al.	206/583
D508,400	S	*	8/2005	Scimone	D9/422
D523,743	S	*	6/2006	Solowiejko et al.	D9/417
D531,025	S	*	10/2006	Tanner	D9/426
7,150,356	B2	*	12/2006	Lofgren et al.	206/583
D535,102	S	*	1/2007	Matsuda	D3/302
D541,045	S		4/2007	Peart et al.	
D554,495	S	*	11/2007	Hanji	D9/418
D554,502	S	*	11/2007	Hoffman et al.	D9/432
7,290,662	B2	*	11/2007	Lofgren et al.	206/583
D557,601	S	*	12/2007	Minidis	D9/425

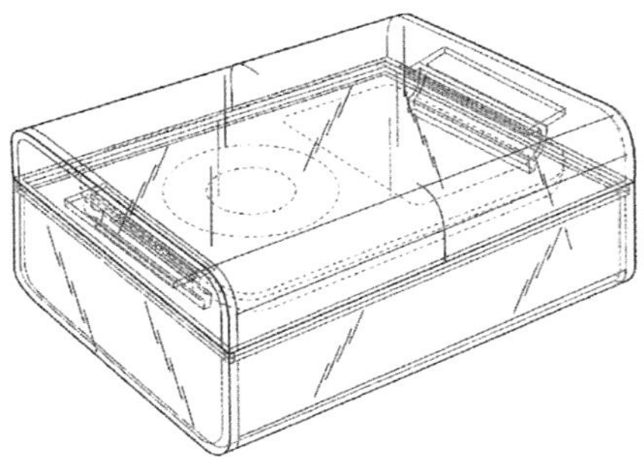

iPod Hi-Fi

AppleTalk Connector Kit
AppleTalk Personal Network

Apple IIe
80-Column Text Card
for IIe only

Macintosh.

iPod
Music
Photos
Extras
Settings
Shuffle Songs
Backlight

$50
iTunes
$25
iTunes
iTunes
iBooks

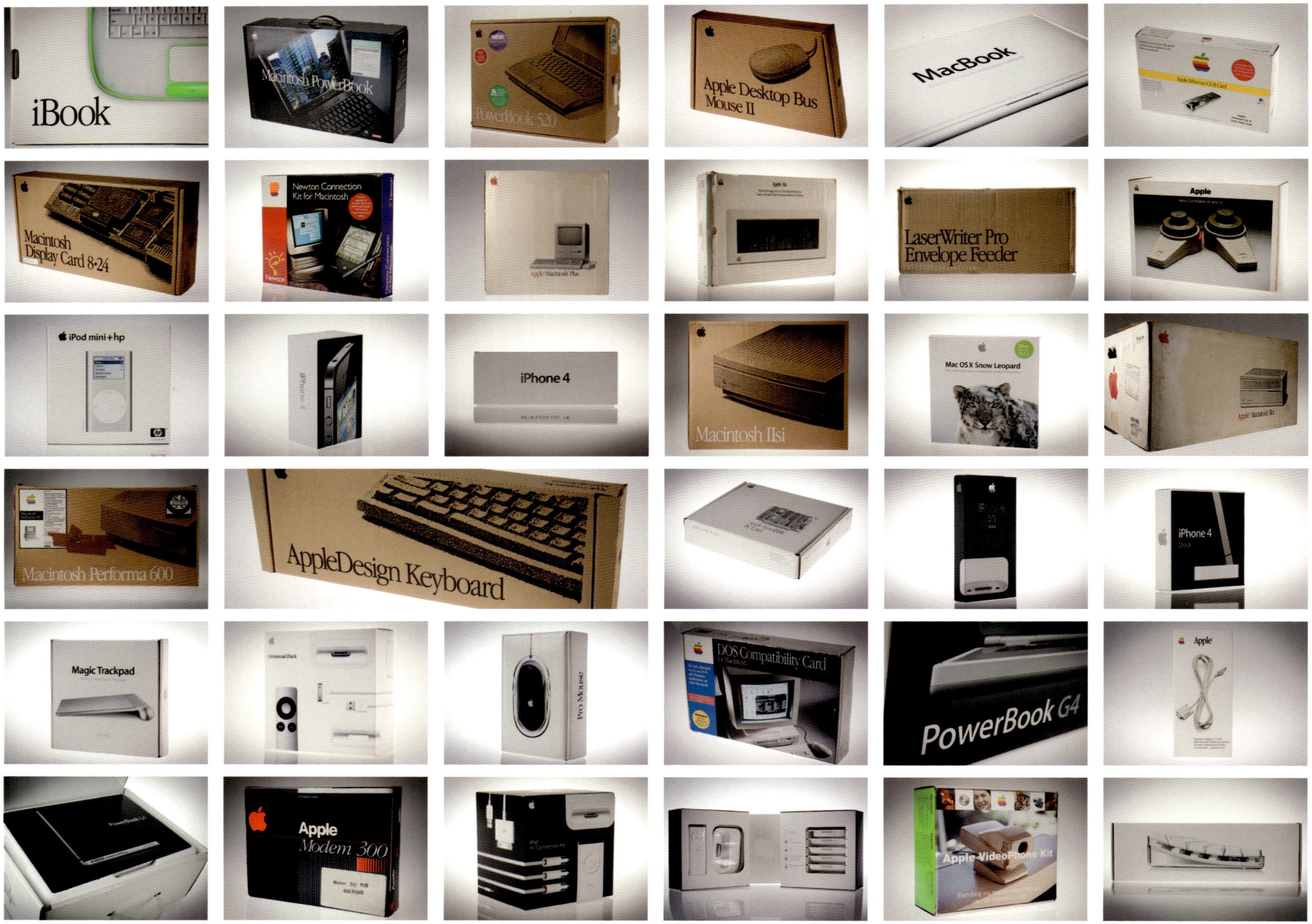
iBook
Macintosh PowerBook
PowerBook 520
Apple Desktop Bus Mouse II
MacBook
Macintosh Display Card 8•24
Newton Connection Kit for Macintosh
LaserWriter Pro Envelope Feeder
Apple
iPod mini + hp
iPhone 4
iPhone 4
Macintosh IIsi
Mac OS X Snow Leopard
Macintosh Performa 600
AppleDesign Keyboard
iPhone 4
Magic Trackpad
Pro Mouse
DOS Compatibility Card
PowerBook G4
Apple
Apple Modem 300
Apple VideoPhone Kit

Apple II
Extended 80-Column Text Card
for IIe only

AppleCD 300

QuickTake 200
Digital Camera
Images limited only by your imagination.

QuickTake 100
Digital Camera for Macintosh
QuickTake 100

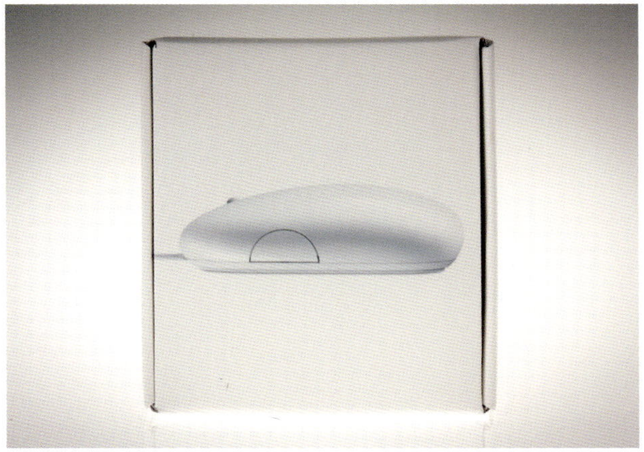

611-0328
EH445H9ZQ40A

Apple VideoPhone Kit

iPod nano
iPod nano
iPod nano
iPod nano
iPod nano

iPod touch
Macy Gray
BIG

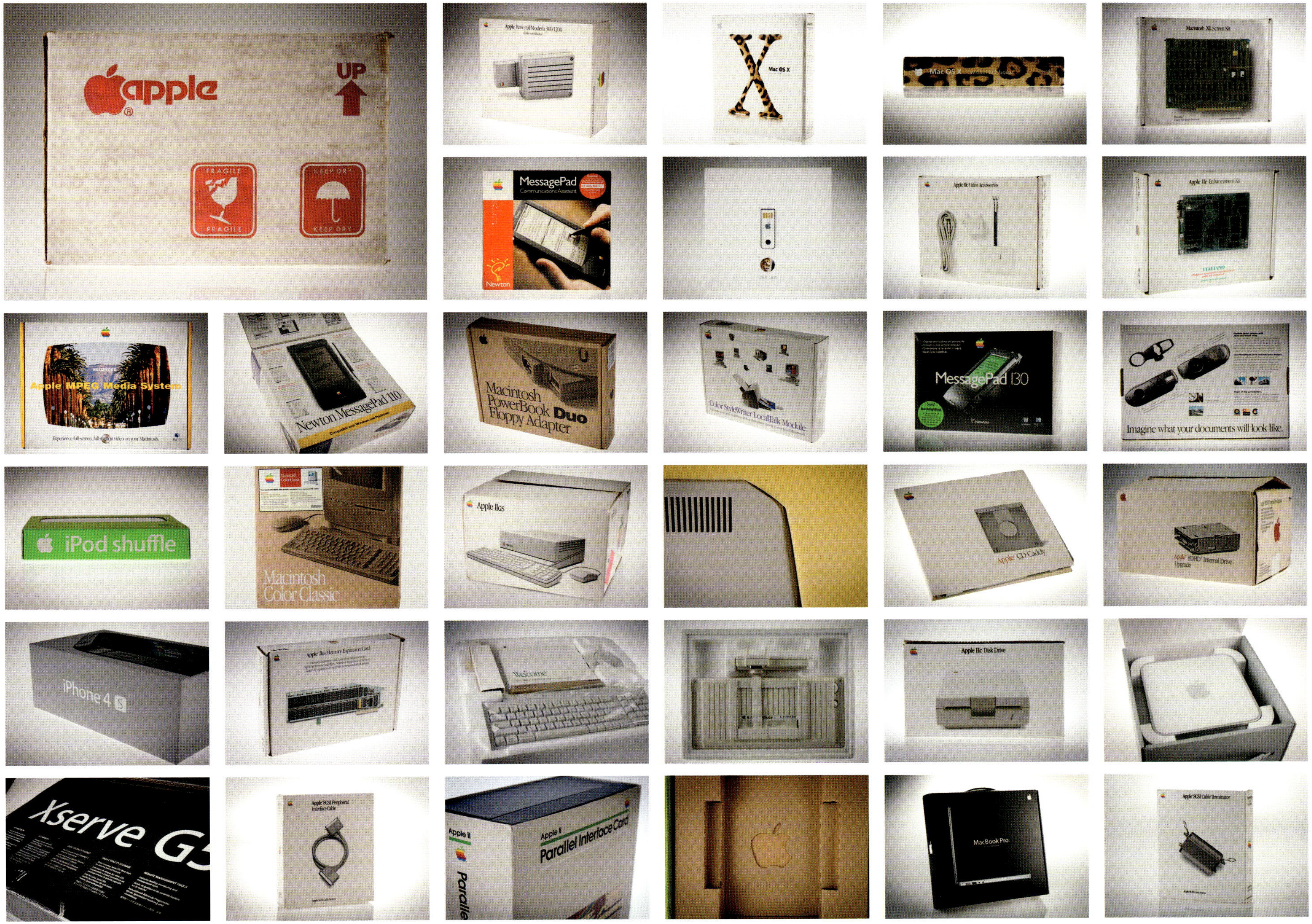
apple
UP
FRAGILE
FRAGILE
KEEP DRY
KEEP DRY
X
MessagePad
Newton
Apple MPEG Media System
Newton MessagePad 110
Macintosh PowerBook Duo Floppy Adapter
MessagePad 130
Imagine what your documents will look like.
iPod shuffle
Macintosh Color Classic
Apple IIgs
iPhone 4 S
Welcome
Xserve G5
Apple II
Parallel Interface Card
MacBook Pro

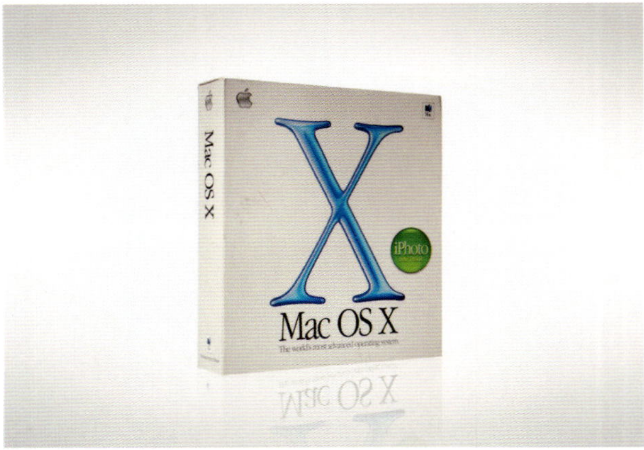
Mac OS X
iPhoto
Mac OS X
The world's most advanced operating system

Mac OS X
Server

Mac OS X

Mac OS X Server
Mac OS X Server

Mac OS X Server

Mac OS X Tiger

Mac OS X Server
Mac OS X Server

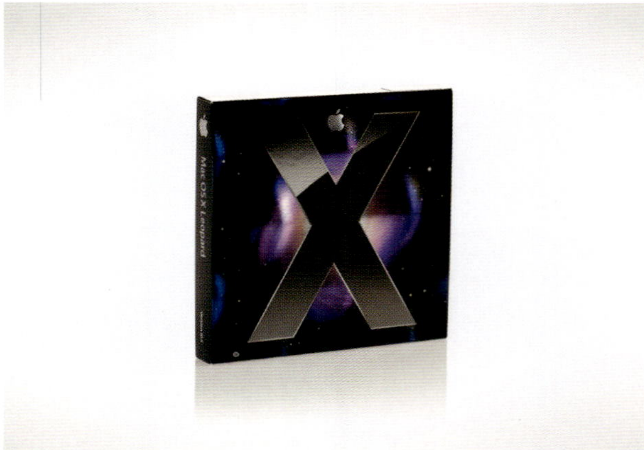
Mac OS X Leopard

Final Cut Server
Media asset management. Workflow automation.

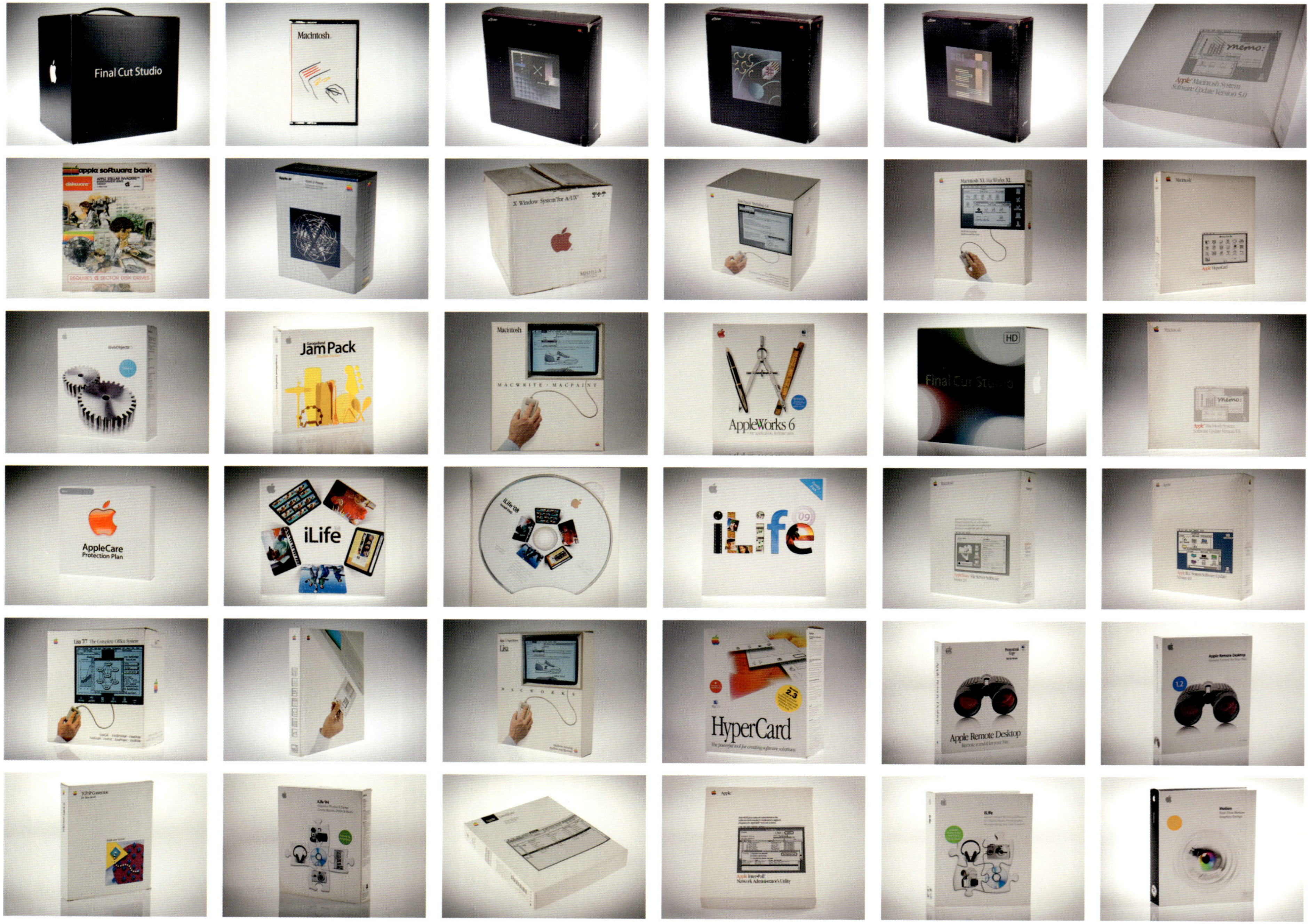
Final Cut Studio
Macintosh
apple software bank
X Window System for A/UX
Jam Pack
Macintosh
AppleWorks 6
HD
AppleCare
Protection Plan
iLife
iLife '09
HyperCard
Apple Remote Desktop

mobile me
Logic Studio
QuickTime
Starter Kit
NEW!
APPLE I MACHINE PROGRAM:
LUNAR LANDER
apple computer inc.
Apple LocalTalk Bridge
AppleShare
Final Cut Pro 2
Apple IIe Tutorial Disks
Mac Box Set
iLife
iWork
Aperture 3
Final Cut Pro 5
Final Cut Studio
Aperture 2
Apple Remote Access
MacProject
MacDraw
Macintosh
System 7
The ideal combination of power and ease of use
Apple Web Page Construction Kit
Final Cut Server
Newton Press
Oracle Power Objects

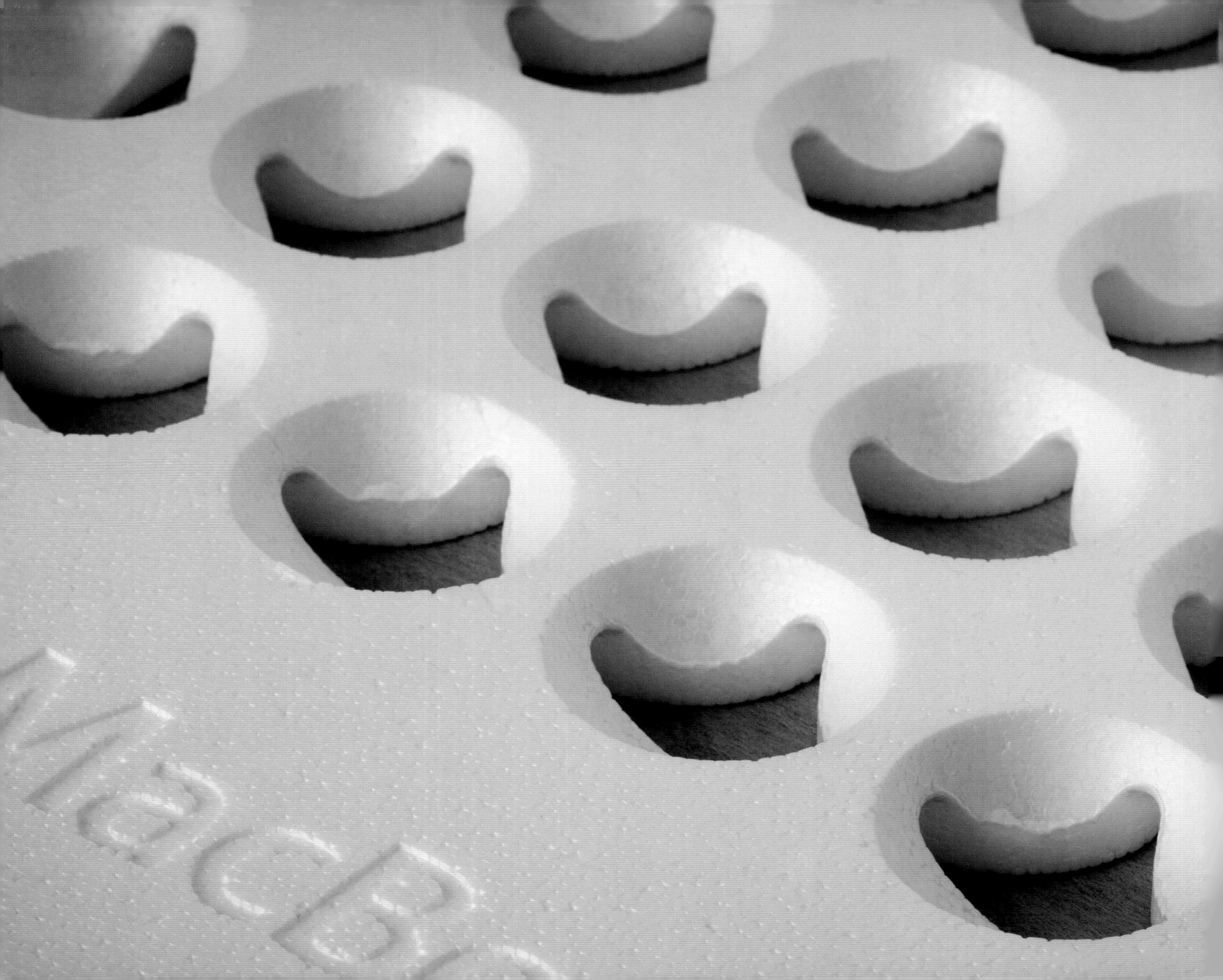

"But we're lucky, because Apple has a purpose. Unlike anyone in the industry, people want us to make products that they love. In fact, more than love. Our job is to make products that people lust for. That's what Apple is meant to be."

—Steve Jobs

10GB
iPod
iPod

iPod
photo 40GB
music+photos Mac+PC
Photo Library

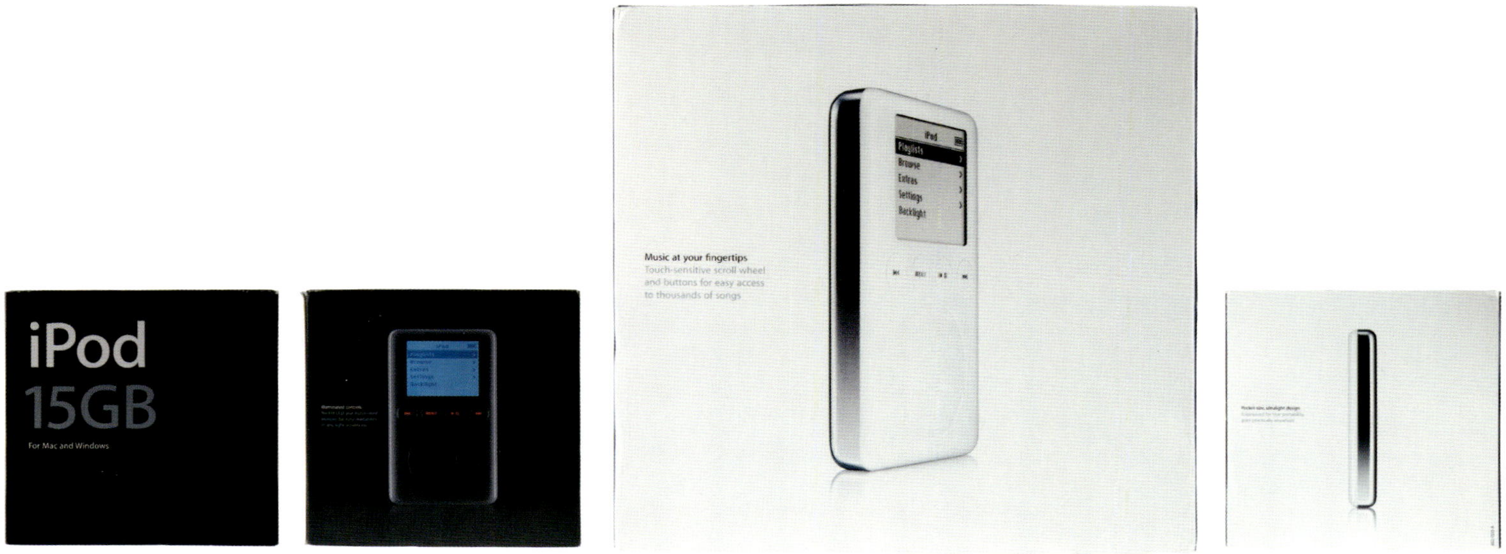

iPod
15GB
For Mac and Windows
Music at your fingertips
Touch-sensitive scroll wheel
and buttons for easy access
to thousands of songs

20GB Mac + PC
iPod
Special Edition
U2

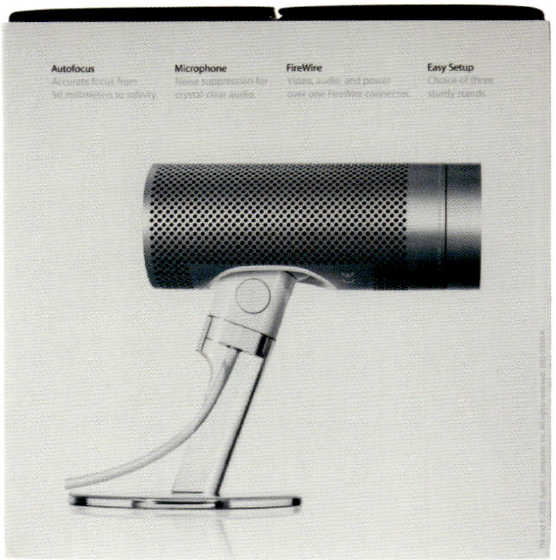
Autofocus
Accurate focus from 50 millimeters to infinity.
Microphone
Noise suppression for crystal clear audio.
FireWire
Video, audio, and power over one FireWire connector.
Easy Setup
Choice of three sturdy stands.

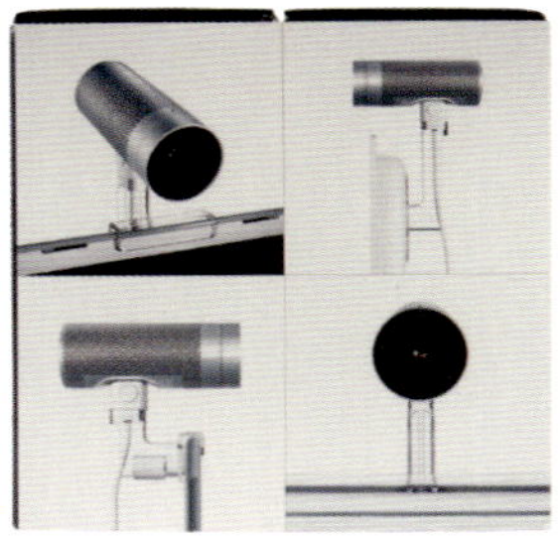

eMac

eMac

eMac

eMac

Organize your business and personal life.
Connect to your personal computer.
MessagePad 120
Expand your capabilities.

MessagePad 120
New!
Newton 2.0
Newton

Organize your business and personal life.
Connect to your personal computer.
MessagePad 130
Expand your capabilities.

MessagePad 130
New!
Backlighting
Newton

iMac
CDRW

iMac

iMac

of 4
Clavier
twentieth anniversary
Macintosh

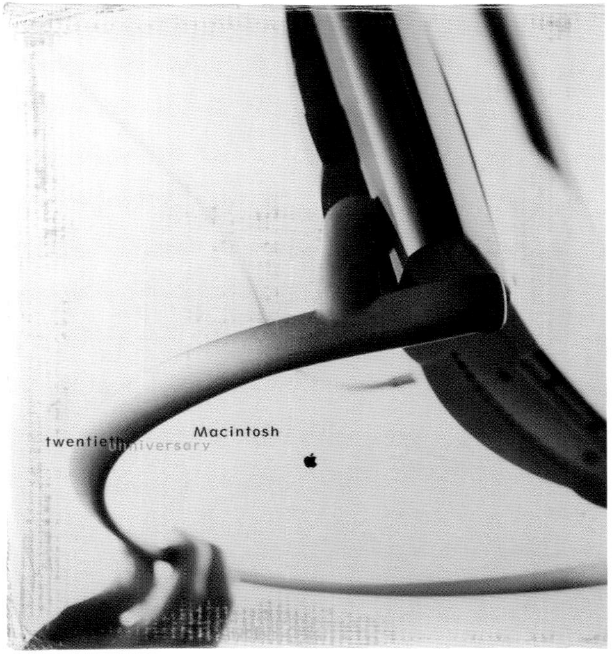
twentieth
Macintosh

Macintosh

Acknowledgments

A project of this size takes a special team, and so I must begin by acknowledging my core team: Forest McMullin and Lisa Clark. My relationship with Forest began the day he tried to teach me how to take a good photo, but it developed into a friendship that made him perfect for the role of photo editor. Forest was the voice of reason through every aspect of the project—his expertise and experience are boundless, and I am grateful to have worked with him on this project. The choice of Lisa Clark as my designer was the right one. Her eye for design is impeccable, and she has showcased my work magnificently. In addition, a special word of gratitude to Shelley Holloway for her keen eye. She is a wonderful copy editor and has helped pull the book together with her invaluable wordsmithing.

Thanks to my two pixel ninjas Kyle Burdg and Kevin Taylor for putting the finishing touches on the photos and making them pop off the page. They are true wizards at their craft, and I couldn't be happier with the results.

I would like to thank John Woodall, a quiet, humble genius of all things Apple, who was so supportive of me from day one. John was instrumental in helping me locate and procure many pre-Macintosh items such as the Lisa and related peripherals. John's knowledge of vintage Apple products, especially the Lisa, is unrivaled. He has also become a good friend.

A special acknowledgment to the Computer History Museum for allowing us to photograph their wonderful specimen of the Macintosh prototype (pages 242-243) The Museum is an amazing facility, and I am proud and honored to be associated with it.

With the exception of the MultiServer, all products in the Prototypes chapter came from private collections. My sincerest thanks to Jim Abeles, Randy Carr, Giuseppe Forello, Gabreal Franklin, Tom Gilley, Daniel Kottke, Lonnie Mimms, and John Woodall. Thank you all for allowing me to capture your treasures on film and highlight them here.

My sincerest thanks to my core contributors Jim Dalrymple, Steve Wozniak, Daniel Kottke, Ken Segall, James Savage, Chet Pipkin, Tom Gilley and Sebastiaan de With. It is an unbelievable honor that these individuals agreed to contribute to my project and their words raised the book to a new level.

My deepest gratitude to the following people for sharing their time, help, thoughts, permissions, memories, ideas, and suggestions for a project created by someone most of you had never met before. Thanks to Adam Berenstain, Loren Brichter, Nolan Bushnell, Dana Carlton, Randy Carr, Nick Chaves, Galvin Collins, George Dick, Benj Edwards, Hartmut Esslinger, Bill Fernandez, Dexter Francis, Alden Haley, Nobuyuki Hayashi, Alex Heath, Ken Hess, Eric Hoffert, Walter Isaacson, Charlie Kindel, Alex Knight, Karen Kroslowitz, Phil Lapsley, Herb Lingl, John McLaughlin, Chris Mealey, Sean Owczarek, Neal A. Pann, Dan Patterson, Kelli Richards, Mark Richards, Michael Rylander, Steve Schaetzel, Dan Sokol, Eric Taylor, Paul Thurrot, Giles Turnbull, and Gary Wolf.

When Jim Dalrymple agreed to write a foreword for *Iconic*, I flew to Nova Scotia to meet him in person. He shared his time, as well as his personal perspective, and I am thankful for both, not to mention the extensive time he invested in writing the foreword. I approached Jim because of his honest, balanced, and thorough reporting of Apple throughout his career, and the enormous respect he draws from the Apple community at large, especially across the broad spectrum of journalists and writers that cover the company. I learned a great deal from Jim in our short time together, and I am very

grateful that he agreed to participate in this project.

In early 2013, as I was putting the finishing touches on *Iconic*, I had the opportunity to show a draft to Steve Wozniak, co-founder of Apple. Sitting with the man who made it all happen was an amazing experience, and he couldn't have been more gracious, energetic, and just plain fun to talk to. As we leafed through the book, every turn of the page triggered another memory, another anecdote or story from his past, or thoughts on the future. It was truly exciting to share my work with a founder of the company, and I'm honored by his contribution to this book.

The project could have never been accomplished without the unwavering support of my friends and family, and the bombardment of direct, personal, non-stop encouragement from Serge Ouanounou, Phil Mekelburg, Aron and Kimberly Levine, Angel and Aaron Goldman, Kevin Warmerdam, Rick Volkmann, Anne Willey, Gary Chapman, Daniel Goodstein, Craig Daitch, Paul Gilliot, Steve Kushner, Mark Wassersug, Scott Wills, Jeremy Weinstein, Joe Barber, Bob Gundeck, Wendy Lauria, Simon Crean, David Aferiat, Jonathan Lerner, Andrew Voznytsa, Dan and Cameron Carter, Jordan Bacon, Chrissy and Eric Curnow, Andrea McMullin, Jeff Collier, Zvi Brooks, Fishel Potash, Joe Chen, Andy Kim, Earnest Winborne, Dave and Rachel Gold, Simon and Simona Weinstein, Joe Ancona, Rupen Dolasia, Fiona, Braham, Dahlia, Benjamin and Jemma Goldberg, Yoram Bercholtz, Natalie and Karl Vogel, Bill and Debbie Liss, Jonathan and Mariel Liss, Bob and Harriet Miller, Ian Miller, Jonas Miller, Jarrod Bernstein and Hildy Kuryk, and Reene Zufi.

To my beautiful wife Louisa and our children—thank you for your incredible patience and support, and for putting up with the continuous stream of boxes blocking the garage and my late night jaunts in the basement. Someday down the road, you will pick up this book and remember why I did this. I hope when you do that you are able to proudly say, "I was there and saw firsthand what can come of having a crazy idea and committing to see it through all the way to the end."

Since launching *Shrine of Apple* (shrineofapple.com), I've amassed a small but loyal group of followers on my social networks. To those Followers and Likers who supported this project from the beginning, to all those people who took the time to contact me to thank me for the site, to offer their help, support, enthusiasm, dedication, and participation—I am truly grateful.

Finally, thank you to the Apple family for all your innovation and ideas. Like the millions of other fans across the globe, I eagerly await the next innovation you have in store for us.

—J. Z.

Contributors

Jim Dalrymple, Founder, Editor in Chief, *The Loop*

Founder of *The Loop*, Jim Dalrymple has been following Apple and its products for the last seventeen years, first as one of the original members of *MacCentral*, then at *Macworld*. He held several positions at *Macworld* over the ten years, including his final job as editor at large, before leaving in May 2009. Jim's work has been in many publications including *Macworld*, *PC World*, *Computerworld*, *Macworld UK* and many others. He's also appeared as an expert on several television stations including CNN, Fox, CBS, and ABC. He continues to do radio show interviews, both Internet-based, like *Your Mac Life* and *MacNotables*, and traditional radio. Jim has been a guitar player for twenty years and records music on his Mac using GarageBand, Logic, Pro Tools, Cubase, Line 6, Native Instruments, IK Multimedia, ToonTrack, FXPansion, and a host of other applications.

Tom Gilley CTO, entrepreneur

Tom Gilley is a technology strategist and entrepreneur with success in social computing, modern media, and mobile technologies. He founded an on-demand web media company which he later sold to Vignette, and as CTO at Vignette, Gilley contributed to company positioning and product strategy, and managed the ultimate sale to OpenText.

Gilley gained his corporate product management experience at Apple Computer. As an engineer and R&D manager in the Advanced Technology Group, he developed and managed an intellectual property portfolio, products and spin-out companies for handheld computers, tablet computers, set-top boxes, media systems, digital cameras, and social computing. Gilley transferred from R&D management to Apple portable product management to lead new-product development.

Before and after Apple, Gilley founded several successful companies including: Meeting Technologies, a social computing company; FutureTel, the first MPEG video broadcast equipment and MPEG2 chip company; and PicoStar, an incubator and technology investment company. At PicoStar, Gilley was the founding CTO for Cobalt Networks, which subsequently sold to Sun for $2 billion. He was also the founding CTO for the second largest news and social portal in Brazil and incubated several Internet technology companies.

Tom lives and works in New York City with professional roots in Silicon Valley.

Daniel Kottke, engineer, entrepreneur

Daniel Kottke was Apple's first employee (part-time, in the garage, in 1976), and rejoined them full time in 1977 after finishing his B.A. in music at Columbia . . . just in time to help out with assembly of the first batch of Apple IIs. A self-taught engineer, during his eight years with Apple, Daniel debugged Apple II printed circuit boards, built Apple III and Macintosh prototypes, and became co-designer of the Macintosh keyboard, with help from Ed Riddle. An original member of the Macintosh development team, his signature can be found on the internal wall of early-production Macintosh computers.

Still a very popular face in the Silicon Valley circles, Daniel continues to invent, engineer, and build new technology products, while also producing and hosting *The Next Step*, a public-access cable television show that reflects his breadth of interests, including technology, the Internet, social networking, spirituality, and various holistic endeavors. Since 2010, Daniel has been very involved in the renovation and re-launch of the dormant Hobergs Resort (aka Maharishi University, 1974–2010), a 125-year-old property in Lake County, California.

Chester (Chet) J. Pipkin, Founder, CEO, Chairman of the Board: Belkin International, Inc.

Born and raised in Southern California, Chet Pipkin has nurtured a lifelong passion for entrepreneurship and innovation, both in building one of the world's most exciting technology brands, and in supporting organizations and individuals that help build and repair the fabric of society for those in need. His story is unique in that his commitment to community, youth, and nonprofit organizations began before he built Belkin into the leading consumer electronics organization we know today.

In the early 1980s, Chet started Belkin in his parents' garage, manufacturing computer cable assemblies in the evenings and on weekends, and selling them to local computer manufacturers and dealers. Some of the very first cables he created were designed to connect Apple-brand computers to external disk drives.

Belkin was founded on Chet's focus on user experience and consumer insights. From the beginning, Chet's product philosophy was inspired by the idea of people using technology to realize their potential. This philosophy aligned well with Apple's own vision of product development. Belkin's commitment to enhancing the user experience has earned it the claim of being one of Apple's largest and most tenured partners in the peripheral ecosystem, and continues to drive the company's success today.

Chet lives in Manhattan Beach, California. He and his wife, Jan, have seven children and two grandchildren.

James Savage, Founder of *RetroMacCast*

James Savage's fascination with Apple and its products began the day his father brought home the family's first computer, an Apple IIe. His interest in computers grew with his first Macintosh which led to a second, a third, and eventually a collection numbering nearly two hundred. He launched *RetroMacCast* in 2006, a weekly podcast in which he and his co-host John discuss Apple's rich history and share their collections with thousands of listeners around the world. His hobby has led to numerous magazine and newspaper articles, speaking engagements, and opportunities to interview other Apple fans and those who helped shape Apple and computing history.

Ken Segall, author, speaker, blogger

Ken is a veteran ad agency creative director who's spent more than half his career creating ads for Steve Jobs and Apple. After working with Apple back in the days of John Scully, Ken spent eight years helping Steve tell the story of NeXT, then came back to the world of Apple when Steve returned from exile in 1997. Ken was a member of the "think different" team and set Apple down the i-path by naming the iMac. His bestselling book, *Insanely Simple: The Obsession That Drives Apple's Success,* is an insider's look at how Steve's love of simplicity helped fuel Apple's spectacular rise. Ken blogs about technology and marketing at kensegall.com and is a co-founder of the popular Apple satire site, scoopertino.com.

Sebastiaan de With, Chief Creative Officer, doubleTwist

Sebastiaan de With loves making and enjoying well-designed things. He strives to make technology better and easier to use through visual and user-interface design.

After receiving and falling in love with his first MacBook Pro, he began digging into what made the "wrapping" of its software so good. The user-interface design captivated him so much that, at age seventeen, he started his own company doing freelance user-interface design, as well as writing detailed user experience breakdowns on his website. He eventually went to work for Steve Jobs in Apple's Internet Services group as essentially half of a two-man design team during Apple's challenging MobileMe to iCloud transition. Since then, Sebastiaan has contributed on teams and led design at companies including HP, Mozilla, and Intel, to name a few. He's also created a website that teaches icon and user interface design to designers and software engineers.

Sebastiaan is a Dutch expatriate, married to his wife Bre and living in San Francisco. He currently serves as chief creative officer at a San Francisco-based startup called doubleTwist, where he's busy creating the new best way to enjoy music, podcasts, and other media.

Steve Wozniak, Co-founder of Apple Inc.

A Silicon Valley icon and philanthropist for the past three decades, Steve helped shape the computing industry with his design of Apple's first line of products. In 1976, Wozniak and Steve Jobs founded Apple Computer Inc. with Wozniak's Apple I personal computer. The following year, he introduced his Apple II personal computer. The Apple II was integral in launching the personal computer industry and began Apple's ascent to be the leader in personal computers, music, and mobile computing.

The Team

Jonathan Zufi
Author and Photographer

Jonathan is the creator of *Iconic*. In 2009, Jonathan conceived the idea of photographing every product ever made by Apple and began showcasing his work on his website *Shrine of Apple* at shrineofapple.com. Jonathan has been a loyal Apple customer since the 1980s and is a veteran of the technology industry. He is a leading expert in mobile software development and currently manages the North American Mobile Innovation Center for SAP. Jonathan's first Apple product was an Apple IIc on which he learned to write software using Logo, Pascal, and Assembly Language.

Forest McMullin
Photo Editor

Forest is a photographer, educator, and consultant to the photographic industry. For over twenty-five years he has specialized in photographing fringe social groups and is respected for his ability to bring out their dignity while still showing them with directness and honesty. He works and exhibits regionally, nationally, and internationally. He regularly conducts workshops and lectures across the United States for a variety of photographic manufacturers. He's currently a Professor of Photography at the Savannah College of Art and Design in Atlanta, Georgia. His first Apple product was a Macintosh Plus he bought in 1987.

Lisa Clark
Designer

Lisa has a twenty-five-year history in design and art direction for a variety of media. Primarily working in print publishing, she was a magazine designer for *Rolling Stone Magazine*, art director for Godine Publishing, book designer for Harvard University Press, and managed the design department at Princeton University Press. Her career includes work in technology as an eBook design manager on the Acrobat team for Adobe Systems. In print and digital, her background has a broad range, always with special attention to typography and photography. Her enthusiasm for Apple products, from her first SE to her current 2012 iMac, has never changed.

Sources

CHAPTER ONE: DESKTOPS

6 Bill Fernandez in discussion with author, August 2012. **8** Robert X. Cringely on PBS NerdTV, September 6, 2005, Interview with Andy Hertzfeld, http://to.pbs.org/10oBkBS **11** Nolan Bushnell in discussion with author, June 2012. **15** Gary Wolf, "The Next Insanely Great Thing," *Wired Magazine*, February 1996, Quote from Steve Jobs, http://bit.ly/ZP1NpU **20** Apple Lisa marketing material, 1982. **22** Bill Fernandez in discussion with author, August 2012. **26** Alex Heath in discussion with author, April 2012. **28** Gabreal Franklin in discussion with author, March 2013. **30** Phil Lemmons, "An Interview: The Macintosh Design Team," *Byte*, Steve Jobs, February 2008 issue, Byte Publications, http://bit.ly/YcJejJ **32** Bill Fernandez in discussion with author, August 2012. **34** Eric Hoffert in discussion with author, June 2012. **39** Walter Isaacson, "How Steve Jobs' Love of Simplicity Fueled A Design Revolution," *Smithsonian*, September 2012, Quote from Jonathan Ive, http://bit.ly/10oBTeY **43** *Design Museum*, 2003, Jonathan Ive Interview, http://bit.ly/ZP23VR **44** Bill Fernandez in discussion with author, August 2012. **47** "Rainbow iMac & Power Mac G3 Introduction – Macworld SF (1999)," YouTube video, 1:39:48, Jonathan Ive, posted by "EverySteveJobsVideo," December 21, 2012, http://bit.ly/163HcSr **49** "Rainbow iMac & Power Mac G3 Introduction – Macworld SF (1999)," YouTube video, 1:39:48, Jonathan Ive, posted by "EverySteveJobsVideo," December 21, 2012, http://bit.ly/163HcSr **50** *Design Museum*, 2003, Jonathan Ive Interview, http://bit.ly/ZP23VR **53** Jonathan Ive. *Objectified*. Directed by Gary Hustwit. Plexifilm, 2009. Documentary DVD. **55** Shane Richmond, "Jonathan Ive interview: simplicity isn't simple," *The Telegraph*, May 23, 2012, http://bit.ly/YrHW1F **56** "Apple's CEO Discusses F1Q 2013 Results – Earnings Call Transcript," Seeking Alpha, January 23, 2013, Quote from Tim Cook, http://bit.ly/100ghEp **58** "Sunflower iMac & iPhoto introduction – Macworld SF (2002)," YouTube video, 1:53:07, Steve Jobs introduces new iMac G4, February 22, 2006, http://bit.ly/Ysc73P **62** David Derbyshire, "His goal was to make it simple to use and a joy to look at. He succeeded. The result was the iPod," *The Telegraph*, Jonathan Ive interview, November 19, 2005, http://bit.ly/YIMVXL **64** "20th Anniversary Macintosh TAM Commercial Report (1997)," YouTube video, 3:31, Jonathan Ive, posted by "sparmtacus," February 19, 2012, http://bit.ly/YIPqt **66** "20th Anniversary Macintosh TAM Commercial Report (1997)," YouTube video, 3:31, Jonathan Ive, posted by "sparmtacus," February 19, 2012, http://bit.ly/YIPqt2 **72** John Gruber, "Redesigned," *Daring Fireball*, August 24, 2011, http://bit.ly/YcYsW0 **77** Kelli Richards, *The Magic and Moxie of Apple – An Insider's View*, [Kindle Edition], All Access Group, June 12, 2012, Appendix A. **78** Dieter Rams. *Objectified*. Directed by Gary Hustwit. Plexfilm, 2009. Documentary DVD. **81** Launch of 2012 iMac, Apple website, http://bit.ly/10sMAtq **83** "Goldman Sachs Technology and Internet Conference," February 12, 2013, Tim Cook, http://bit.ly/15x1BgG

CHAPTER TWO: PORTABLES

87 Jean-Louis Gassée at 1989 launch of the Macintosh Portable. **90** Josh Tyrangiel, "Tim Cook's Freshman Year: The Apple CEO Speaks," *BloombergBusinessweek*, December 6, 2012, Quote from Tim Cook, http://buswk.co/WOLknW **95** Jonathan Ive. *Objectified*. Directed by Gary Hustwit. Plexifilm, 2009. Documentary DVD. **102** Steven Levy, *Insanely Great: The Life and Times of Macintosh, the Computer that Changed Everything* (Penguin Books 2000), 261. **104** "Apple iBook – First Impressions (1999)," YouTube video, 4:02, Jonathan Ive, posted by "vintagemacmusum," May 23, 2011, http://bit.ly/ZXvV11 **109** "Original iBook, AirPort & HALO introduction – Macworld NY (1999)," YouTube video, 1:17:02, Steve Jobs, posted by "EverySteveJobsVideo," January 30, 2006, http://bit.ly/ZP7CUc **111** *Design Museum*, 2003, Interview with Jonathan Ive, http://bit.ly/ZP23VR **114** Jonathan Ive. *Objectified*. Directed by Gary Hustwit. Plexifilm, 2009. Documentary DVD. **118** Christopher Stringer, Apple Samsung Trial, July 2012. **121** "The Demo That Changed The World," YouTube video, 13:53, Jonathan Ive, episode of *Genius of Design*, posted by "555topcats," April 9, 2011, http://bit.ly/13gNNLT **122** Ken Segall in discussion with author, September 2012. **124** "Apple WWDC 2012 Keynote Address," iTunes video, 1 hr 54 min, Bob Mansfield, posted by Apple Inc., June 11, 2012, http://itun.es/i6JN8dL **126** "Macworld San Francisco 2008 Keynote Address," iTunes video, 1 hr 16 min, Steve Jobs, posted by Apple Inc., January 16, 2008, http://itun.es/i6JN9bw

CHAPTER THREE: PERIPHERALS

138 "Goldman Sachs Technology and Internet Conference," Tim Cook, February 12, 2013, http://bit.ly/15x1BgG **146** "NEW Apple Magic Mouse with Multi touch," YouTube video, 1:25, Jonathan Ive, posted by "Kirpitch TV," October 21, 2009, http://bit.ly/ZCEyjG **149** "Goldman Sachs Technology and Internet Conference," Tim Cook, February 12, 2013, http://bit.ly/15x1BgG **163** *Design Museum*, 2003, Jonathan Ive Interview, http://bit.ly/ZP23VR **164** "Apple WWDC 2003," YouTube video, 2:05:51, Steve Jobs talks about the camera, posted by "AppleVideoArchive," December 31, 2011, http://bit.ly/ZYamNG **165** "Apple WWDC 2003," YouTube video, 2:05:51, Steve Jobs talks about the camera, posted by "AppleVideoArchive," December 31, 2011, http://bit.ly/ZYamNG **166** "Apple WWDC 2012 Keynote Address", iTunes video, Jonathan Ive talks about the Retina MacBook Pro, posted by Apple Inc., June 11, 2012, http://itun.es/i6JN9mx **174** Matt Warman, "Dieter Rams: Apple has achieved something I never did," *The Telegraph*, June 4, 2011, http://bit.ly/ZXzyDW **181** Charlie Kindel, "Why Nobody Can Copy Apple," cek.log, February 19, 2013, http://bit.ly/16M3CJn **182** Nick Chaves, "Hackers gonna hate," NickChaves.com, June 17, 2012, http://bit.ly/13gkDMH **184** "Apple Special Event, September 2012," iTunes video, 1 hr 45 min, EarPod introduction—Jonathan Ive, posted by Apple Inc., September 12, 2012, http://itun.es/i6Jn96g

CHAPTER FOUR: iDEVICES

188 Steven Levy, "Steve Jobs, 1955 – 2011," *Wired* online magazine, October 5, 2011, 7:58 pm, Quote from Steve Jobs, http://bit.ly/ZBVeaZ **191** Hartmut Esslinger, *DESIGN FORWARD: Creative Strategies for Sustainable Change* (Stuttgart, Germany: ARNOLDSCHE Art Publishers 2013) 34. **193** "Original iPod introduction – Apple Special Event (2001)," YouTube video, 50:11, Jonathan Ive talks about the iPod, posted by "EverySteveJobsVideo," http://bit.ly/16Ml94f **195** M.G. Siegler, "One More Thing..." *TechCrunch*, August 26, 2011, http://tcrn.ch/14aCljX **196** "Original iPod introduction – Apple Special Event (2001)," YouTube video, 50:11, Moby talks about the iPod, posted by "EverySteveJobsVideo," http://bit.ly/16Ml94f **198** Josh Tyrangiel, "Tim Cook's Freshman Year: The Apple CEO Speaks," *BloombergBusinessweek*, December 6, 2012, Quote from Tim Cook, http://buswk.co/WOLknW **201** Kelli Richards, *The Magic and Moxie of Apple – An Insider's View*, [Kindle Edition], All Access Group, June 12, 2012, Chapter 6. **202** Jonathan Ive. *Objectified*. Directed by Gary Hustwit. Plexifilm, 2009. Documentary DVD. **206** Josh Tyrangiel, "Tim Cook's Freshman Year: The Apple CEO Speaks," *BloombergBusinessweek*, December 6, 2012, Quote from Tim Cook, http://buswk.co/WOLknW **208** "iPod nano & Motorola ROKR introduction – Apple Special Music Event (2005)," YouTube video, 46:11, Steve Jobs introduces iPod nano, posted by "EverySteveJobsVideo," December 21, 2012, http://bit.ly/14aC54E **211** Ken Segall in discussion with author, September 2012. **212** Nobuyuki "Nobi" Hayashi in discussion with author, September 2012. **213** Hartmut Esslinger, *DESIGN FORWARD: Creative Strategies for Sustainable Change* (Stuttgart, Germany: ARNOLDSCHE Art Publishers 2013) 10. **214** Ken Segall in discussion with author, September 2012. **217** Paul Thurrot, "Compete Report: iPod nano (Late 2012)," Paul Thurrott's Supersite for Windows, October 17, 2012, http://bit.ly/ZPc6KD **224** "Macworld San Francisco 2007 Keynote Address," iTunes video, 1 hr 45 min, Steve Jobs kicks off Macworld 2007, posted by Apple Inc., January 9, 2007, http://itun.es/i6Jn9DK **226** Judgment by His Honour Judge Birss QC, in the case of Samsung Electronics (UK) Limited and Apple Inc., Case No HC 11 C 03050, 09/07/2012, pg 37, Item 182. http://bit.ly/10nNNDF **228** Loren Brichter in discussion with author, January 2013. **231** "Apple Special Event, September 2012," iTunes video, 1 hr 45 min, iPhone 5 introduction—Bob Mansfield, posted by Apple Inc., September 12, 2012, http://itun.es/i6Jn96g **232** "Apple Announces iPad," iTunes video, 1 hr 33 min, Steve Jobs, posted by Apple Inc., January 27, 2010, http://itun.es/i6JN9br **234** "Apple Announces iPad," iTunes video, 1 hr 33 min, Jonathan Ive, posted by Apple Inc., January 27, 2010, http://itun.es/i6JN9br **236** "Apple Special Event, October 2012," iTunes video, 1 hr 12 min, Jonathan Ive on the iPad mini, posted by Apple Inc., October 23, 2012, http://itun.es/i6JN8dP

CHAPTER FIVE: PROTOTYPES

241 "Steve Jobs: Secrets of Life," YouTube video, 1:43, Silicon Valley Historical video, posted by "SCVHA," October 6, 2011, http://bit.ly/ZgdUtR **244** Jean-Louis Gassée, at 1989 launch of the Macintosh Portable. **248** Neal A. Pann in discussion with author, May 2012. **254** Shane Richmond, "Jonathan Ive interview: simplicity isn't simple," *The Telegraph*, May 23, 2012, http://bit.ly/YrHW1F **261** Adam Tow, "Steve Jobs Was Technology's Change Agent," Tow.com, October 9, 2011, eMate quote from Steve Jobs, http://bit.ly/13gj5lO **264** Ken Hess, "If you think Apple competes with Android, you're wrong," *ZDNet*, June 21, 2012, http://zd.net/11lRmLF **271** Ken Segall, in discussion with author, September 2012. **272** Randy Carr, in discussion with author, October 2012. **274** "Apple Special Event, October 2008," iTunes video, 52 sec, Jonathan Ive, launch of MacBook Pro 2008, posted by Apple Inc., October 14, 2008, http://itun.es/i6Jn9Jm **277** Kelli Richards, *The Magic and Moxie of Apple – An Insider's View*, [Kindle Edition], All Access Group, June 12, 2012, Chapter 2.

CHAPTER SIX: PACKAGING

284 Josh Tyrangiel, "Tim Cook's Freshman Year: The Apple CEO Speaks," *BloombergBusinessweek*, December 6, 2012, Quote from Tim Cook, http://buswk.co/WOLknW **311** Adam Nash, "Steve Jobs, BMW & eBay," *Psychohistory*, October 10, 2011, http://bit.ly/Z1YX2B

Iconic was set in Kepler and Avenir typefaces.

Named after the German Renaissance astronomer, Kepler is a contemporary type family created by Adobe type designer Robert Slimbach in the tradition of classic modern 18th-century typefaces. Avenir was designed in 1988 by Adrian Frutiger. The word "avenir" means "future" in French and implies an interpretation of Futura. All photographs in *Iconic* were taken with a combination of the following cameras: Canon XSi, Canon 5D Mark II, Nikon D2X, and Nikon D600. The lighting equipment included strobes by Alien Bee and Elinchrom. The majority of the photographs were shot on the Manfrotto Large Still Life Shooting Table. The book was printed on GoldEast Matte paper.

Thank you.